GREAT TASTES

VEGETARIAN

First published in 2009 by Bay Books, an imprint of Murdoch Books Pty Limited
This edition published in 2010.

Murdoch Books Australia
Pier 8/9
23 Hickson Road
Millers Point NSW 2000
Phone: +61 (0) 2 8220 2000
Fax: +61 (0) 2 8220 2558
www.murdochbooks.com.au

Murdoch Books UK Limited
Erico House, 6th Floor
93–99 Upper Richmond Road
Putney, London SW15 2TG
Phone: +44 (0) 20 8785 5995
Fax: +44 (0) 20 8785 5985
www.murdochbooks.co.uk

Chief Executive: Juliet Rogers
Publishing Director: Kay Scarlett
Publisher: Lynn Lewis
Senior Designer: Heather Menzies
Designer: Wendy Inkster
Production: Kita George

ISBN: 9780681657816

PRINTED IN CHINA

IMPORTANT: Those who might be at risk from the effects of salmonella poisoning (the elderly, pregnant women, young children and those suffering from immune deficiency diseases) should consult their doctor with any concerns about eating raw eggs.

OVEN GUIDE: You may find cooking times vary depending on the oven you are using. For fan-forced ovens, as a general rule, set the oven temperature to 20°C (35°F) lower than indicated in the recipe.

Great Tastes: Vegetarian features recipes that include dairy, fish and eggs. It is not designed for strict vegetarians and vegans.

GREAT TASTES

VEGETARIAN

More than 120 easy recipes for every day

bay books

CONTENTS

DIPS & SPREADS

CAPSICUM, CHILLI AND SEMI-DRIED TOMATO SPREAD

MAKES 500 ML (17 FL OZ/2 CUPS)

1 large red capsicum (pepper),
  seeded and quartered

90 g (3¼ oz/½ cup) semi-dried
  (sun-blushed) tomatoes

2 teaspoons sambal oelek (see Note)

125 g (4½ oz/½ cup) spreadable
  cream cheese

2 tablespoons chopped basil

pitta bread, toasted and cut into fingers,
  to serve

1 **Preheat the grill (broiler)** to high. Arrange the capsicum, skin side up, on a wire rack and grill (broil) for 10 minutes, or until well blackened. Cool in a plastic bag, then peel and discard the skin. Chop the flesh.

2 **Drain the semi-dried tomatoes** well on paper towels, pat dry and roughly chop. Put in a small processor fitted with the metal blade and add the capsicum, sambal oelek, cream cheese and basil. Whizz for 10 seconds, or until roughly combined. The tomatoes should still have some texture. Season well with salt and freshly ground black pepper.

3 **Serve the spread** on toasted pitta bread fingers, or other breads and biscuits. It also goes well with boiled or roasted new potatoes. You can store the spread, covered, in the refrigerator for up to 5 days.

Note: Sambal oelek is a paste made from ground red chillies, sometimes including salt, lime or lemongrass as well. Used for adding heat to dishes without altering the other flavours. Sambal oelek can be made from raw ingredients or purchased ready-made.

SPINACH PÂTÉ

MAKES 1½ CUPS

400 g English spinach

30 g (1 oz) butter

½ teaspoon ground coriander (cilantro)

pinch cayenne pepper

2 spring onions, roughly chopped

1 clove garlic

⅓ cup (50 g/1¾ oz) blanched almonds

2 teaspoons white wine vinegar

½ cup (125 g/4½ oz) sour cream

pitta bread, toasted and cut into fingers,
    to serve

1 **Remove the stems** from the spinach. Wash the leaves and place wet in a pan. Cover and cook for 2 minutes, or until wilted, then drain, reserving ¼ cup (60 ml) of the cooking liquid. Cool the spinach then squeeze dry.

2 **Melt the butter** in a small pan. Add the coriander, cayenne pepper, spring onion, garlic and almonds, and cook until the onion is tender. Remove from heat and cool.

3 **Place in a** food processor and process until finely chopped. Add the spinach and process, gradually adding the reserved cooking liquid and vinegar.

4 **Stir in the sour cream** and season well with salt and freshly ground black pepper.

5 **Serve with pitta bread wedges,** savoury crackers or crusty bread.

LA CAPRIATA

SERVES 4

150 g (5½ oz/1 cup) dried broad (fava) beans

4 garlic cloves

1 tablespoon rosemary, roughly chopped

2 teaspoons tomato paste (concentrated purée)

pinch of cayenne pepper

1 tablespoon lemon juice

60 ml (2 fl oz/¼ cup) extra virgin olive oil

¼ teaspoon sesame oil

extra cayenne pepper, to garnish

fresh pitta bread, to serve

1 **Put the broad beans** in a large bowl and cover with cold water. Leave to soak overnight, uncovered. Drain, rinse under cold water and put in a large saucepan with two of the garlic cloves. Cover with plenty of cold water and bring to the boil. Reduce the heat to low and simmer for 1 hour, or until tender.

2 **Drain the broad beans** and transfer to a blender or small processor fitted with the metal blade.

3 **Chop the remaining garlic cloves** and add to the processor, along with the rosemary, tomato paste, cayenne pepper and lemon juice. Whizz for 12–15 seconds, or until finely chopped.

4 **Add the oils** and whizz to combine, then season well with salt and freshly ground black pepper. Spoon into a serving dish, cover and chill for 24 hours.

5 **Remove the spread** from the refrigerator and bring to room temperature. Sprinkle the surface with cayenne pepper.

6 **Serve with fresh pitta** bread cut into triangles or celery stalks or fresh carrot sticks.

SWEET POTATO AND RED LENTIL DIP

SERVES 6–8

250 g (9 oz) orange sweet potato, roughly chopped

1 tablespoon olive oil

1 small red onion, finely chopped

1 garlic clove, crushed

1 teaspoon grated fresh ginger

1 tablespoon Thai red curry paste

200 g (7 oz) tinned chopped tomatoes

125 g (4½ oz/½ cup) whole red lentils, rinsed (see Note)

375 ml (13 fl oz/1½ cups) chicken stock

pitta bread wedges, savoury crackers or crusty bread, to serve

1   Put the sweet potato in a steamer and cover with a lid. Sit the steamer over a wok or saucepan of boiling water and steam for 15 minutes, or until tender. Transfer to a bowl, cool and mash roughly with a fork.

2   Heat the oil in a saucepan over a medium heat and cook the onion for 2 minutes, or until softened.

3   Add the garlic, ginger and curry paste and stir for 30 seconds.

4   Add the tomatoes, lentils and stock to the pan. Bring to the boil, then reduce the heat to low, cover and simmer, stirring often, for 30 minutes, or until the mixture thicken and the lentils have softened but are still intact.

5   Spoon mixture into a bowl, refrigerate until cold, then carefully mix into the mashed sweet potato. Season to taste with salt and freshly ground black pepper.

6   Serve with pitta bread wedges, savoury crackers or crusty bread for dipping.

Note: If you are using split red lentils for this recipe, reduce the cooking time to 10–15 minutes and don't cover with a lid.

ROAST GARLIC AND ARTICHOKE SPREAD ON PIADINI

SERVES 4

PIADINI

250 g (9 oz/2 cups) plain
  (all-purpose) flour

60 ml (2 fl oz/¼ cup) milk

60 ml (2 fl oz/¼ cup) olive oil

1 teaspoon salt

80 ml (2½ fl oz/⅓ cup) water

SPREAD

1 garlic bulb

olive oil spray

400 g (14 oz) tin artichoke hearts
  in brine, drained

3 tablespoons chopped flat-leaf (Italian)
  parsley

2 tablespoons olive oil

1 **To make the piadini,** put the flour in a small processor fitted with the plastic blade. Add the milk, oil, salt and water. Whizz until a smooth, slightly sticky ball forms, adding a little more water if needed. Turn out onto a floured surface and knead for 10 minutes, or until elastic. Cut the dough into three pieces. Cover with plastic wrap and set aside for at least 20 minutes. Roll each piece of dough into a 23 cm (9 inch) disc, 2 mm (1/16 inch) thick.

2 **Slowly heat** a large cast-iron skillet or heavy-based frying pan over low heat until very hot. Add one of the dough discs and cook for 20 seconds, then turn and cook the other side for 20 seconds. Prick all over with a fork, then cook, turning frequently, for a further 3–4 minutes, or until the dough is dry and white, but mottled with burn marks. Transfer to a wire rack to cool. Repeat with the remaining dough discs.

3 **To make the spread,** preheat oven to 180°C (350°F/Gas 4). Spray the garlic with oil, then wrap in foil. Bake for 30 minutes, or until soft. Set aside to cool, then squeeze the garlic flesh into a bowl. Gently squeeze the excess water from the artichokes, then cut them in half. Pat the artichokes dry with paper towels and spray well with oil. Heat a chargrill pan to very hot. Add the artichokes and cook, turning often, for about 3 minutes, or until browned. Put the artichokes, garlic purée, parsley and oil in the processor fitted with the metal blade. Season well with salt and freshly ground black pepper and whizz for about 12 seconds, or until roughly blended.

4 **Cut the piadini** into wedges and coat thickly with the spread.

Note: The piadini can be reheated in a 200°C (400°F/Gas 6) oven for 5 minutes.

MOROCCAN SWEET CARROT AND HONEY DIP

SERVES 6

150 g (5 oz) chickpeas

50 g (1¾ oz) butter

½ teaspoon gound cumin

½ teaspoon ground coriander

½ teaspoon ground cinnamon

¼ teaspoon chilli powder

200 g (6 oz) carrots, chopped

1 tablespoon honey

80 g (2¾ oz/⅓ cup) thick natural yoghurt

2 tablespoons chopped parsely

2 tablespoons olive oil

1 tablespoon olive oil, extra

celery sticks or corn chips or tortilla chips, to serve

1 Put the chickpeas in a bowl, cover with water and leave overnight to rehydrate.

2 Place the chickpeas in a saucepan and cover with cold water, bring to the boil, reduce the heat and simmer for 45 minutes or until tender. Skim off any scum that rises to the surface. Drain, rinse, and mash well.

3 Melt the butter in a heavy-based frying pan. Add the cumin, coriander, cinnamon, chilli and carrots. Cook, covered, over low heat for 5 minutes, turning the carrots to coat them in the spices. Drizzle with honey. If the carrots start to stick add 1 tablespoon of water. Cover and cook for 20 minutes until the carrots are very tender and a caramel brown colour. Cool slightly and mash in the frying pan to keep all the pan juices.

4 Combine the mashed chickpeas and carrot, with the yoghurt, parsley and olive oil, and season well with freshly ground black pepper and salt.

5 Spoon into a serving bowl and drizzle with extra oil. Serve with celery sticks or corn chips or tortilla chips.

Note: If you use canned chickpeas (half a 300 g can chickpeas, drained) the cooking time will be much shorter but the flavour not quite as good.

MUSHROOM PÂTÉ ON CROSTINI

SERVES 4

4 slices white bread, crusts removed

1 tablespoon olive oil

1 onion, chopped

2 garlic cloves, chopped

325 g (12 oz) flat mushrooms, chopped

125 ml (4 fl oz/½ cup) white wine

2 tablespoons thyme

4 tablespoons chopped parsley

2 tablespoons lemon juice, or to taste

1 tablespoon pouring cream

CROSTINI

1 small baguette, thinly sliced on the diagonal

olive oil spray

2 garlic cloves, halved

1 **Whizz the bread** in a small processor fitted with the metal blade for 20 seconds, or until it forms breadcrumbs. You will need 80 g (2¾ oz/1 cup) of breadcrumbs.

2 **Heat the oil** in a deep-sided frying pan over medium heat. Add the onion and garlic and cook for 2 minutes.

3 **Add the mushrooms,** wine and thyme, cover and simmer, stirring once or twice, for 10 minutes. Remove the lid and allow any liquid to evaporate. Set aside to cool a little.

4 **Put the mushroom mixture,** breadcrumbs, parsley, lemon juice and cream in the processor and whizz for 30 seconds, or until finely chopped. Add more lemon juice, to taste, and season well with salt and freshly ground black pepper. Cover and refrigerate for at least 1 hour.

5 **To make the crostini,** preheat the oven to 180°C (350°F/ Gas 4). Lightly spray each side of the baguette slices with oil and arrange on a large baking tray. Bake, turning once, for 12–15 minutes, or until crisp and golden. Rub each crostini with the cut surface of the garlic.

6 **Serve** the crostini spread with the mushroom pâté.

Note: Store the pate, covered, in the refrigerator for up to 5 days.

BROAD BEAN DIP

SERVES 6

175 g (6 oz/1¼ cups) dried broad (fava) beans or ready-skinned dried broad beans

2 garlic cloves, crushed

½ tablespoons ground cumin

1½ tablespoons lemon juice

80 ml (2½ fl oz/⅓ cup) olive oil

large pinch of paprika

2 tablespoons chopped flat-leaf (Italian) parsley

flat bread, to serve

1 Put the dried broad beans in a large bowl, cover with 750 ml (26 fl oz/3 cups) cold water and leave to soak in a cool place. If using dried beans with skins, soak them for 48 hours, changing the water once. If using ready-skinned dried beans, soak them for 12 hours only.

2 Drain the beans. If using beans with skins, remove the skins. To do this, slit the skin with the point of a knife and slip the bean out of its skin.

3 Put the beans in a large saucepan with water to cover and bring to the boil. Cover and simmer over low heat for 1 hour, or until tender (if the water boils over, uncover the pan a little). After 1 hour, remove the lid and cook for a further 15 minutes, or until most of the liquid has evaporated, taking care that the beans do not catch on the base of the pan.

4 Purée the beans in a food processor, then transfer to a bowl and stir in the garlic, cumin and lemon juice. Add salt, to taste.

5 Gradually stir in enough olive oil to give a spreadable or thick dipping consistency, starting with half the oil. As the mixture cools it may become thicker, in which case you can stir through a little warm water to return the mixture to a softer consistency.

6 Spread the purée over a large dish and sprinkle with paprika and parsley. Serve with flat bread of your choice.

ROASTED EGGPLANT DIP

SERVES 4

1 large eggplant (aubergine)

2 teaspoons ground cumin

1 garlic clove, crushed

juice of ½ lemon

2 tablespoons extra virgin olive oil

2 tablespoons chopped coriander (cilantro) leaves

Lebanese bread, to serve

1   **Preheat the oven** to 220°C (425°F/Gas 7). Prick the eggplant several times with a fork and put on a baking tray. Bake for 40–50 minutes, or until the skin is wrinkled and the eggplant appears collapsed. Remove from the oven and set aside to cool.

2   **Dry-fry the cumin** in a frying pan over medium heat for 1–2 minutes, or until the colour deepens and the cumin gives off its fragrant aroma. Set aside to cool.

3   **Cut open the eggplant,** scoop the flesh into a sieve and drain for 5 minutes. Chop the eggplant flesh until finely diced.

4   **Put into a bowl** and stir in the cumin, garlic, lemon juice, oil, and coriander and season with salt and freshly ground black pepper to taste.

5   **Grill (broil) the Lebanese bread,** cut into fingers and serve with the dip.

CHILLI CON QUESO WITH POTATO SKINS

POTATO SKINS

6 large potatoes, skin on, brushed

oil, for deep-frying

CHILLI CON QUESO

30 g (1 oz) butter

½ red onion, finely chopped

2 jalapeño chillies

1 garlic clove, crushed

½ teaspoon Hungarian sweet paprika

1½ tablespoons Mexican beer

125 g (4½ oz/½ cup) sour cream

200 g (7 oz) cheddar cheese, grated

1 tablespoon chopped coriander
(cilantro) leaves

1 To make potato skins, preheat the oven to hot 210°C (415°F/Gas 6–7). Prick each potato with a fork and bake for 1 hour, or until the skins are crisp and the flesh is soft. Turn once during cooking. Leave the potatoes to cool, then halve them and scoop out the flesh, leaving a thin layer of potato in each shell. Cut each half into 3 wedges. Fill a deep heavy-based pan one-third full of oil and heat to 190°C (375°F) or until a cube of bread browns in 10 seconds. Cook the potato skins in batches for 2–3 minutes, or until crisp. Drain on paper towels. Sprinkle with salt and freshly ground black pepper.

2 While the potatoes are cooking, roast the chillies by holding them with tongs (one at a time) over a gas flame, until well blackened (or, if you don't have gas, cut the chillies in half, remove the seeds, flatten out and grill (broil) until the skin turns black). Place in a plastic bag and set aside to cool. Scrape away the skin, remove the seeds and finely chop the flesh.

3 Melt the butter in a saucepan over medium heat. Add the onion and cook for 5 minutes, or until softened. Increase the heat to high, add the chillies, garlic and paprika, and stir for 1 minute to combine.

4 Add the beer, bring to the boil and cook until almost evaporated. Reduce the heat to low and add the sour cream, stirring until smooth.

5 Add the cheese and stir until the cheese is just melted and the mixture is smooth. Remove from the heat, stir through the coriander, and season to taste. Serve warm with potato skins.

Note: The chilli con queso can also be served with corn or tortilla chips for dipping.

STARTERS

SAN CHOY BAU

SERVES 4

8 large iceberg lettuce leaves

6 dried shiitake mushrooms

1 tablespoon dark soy sauce

2 tablespoons hoisin sauce

2 tablespoons Chinese rice wine

½ teaspoon sugar

½ teaspoon sesame oil

1 teaspoon cornflour (cornstarch), mixed with 1 teaspoon cold water

1 tablespoon vegetable or peanut oil

5 spring onions (scallions), finely chopped

2 garlic cloves, crushed

1 tablespoon finely grated fresh ginger

2 tablespoons finely chopped coriander (cilantro) stems

125 g (4½ oz) packet fried tofu puffs, shredded

300 g (10½ oz/4 cups) shredded cabbage

110 g (3¾ oz/⅔ cup) drained water chestnuts, chopped

1 handful coriander (cilantro) leaves

2 spring onions (scallions), extra, sliced on the diagonal, to serve

hoisin sauce, extra, to serve

1 **Wash the lettuce,** dry well and set aside until needed.

2 **Soak the shiitake mushrooms** in 125 ml (4 fl oz/½ cup) of hot water for 10 minutes. Drain the mushrooms, reserving 2 tablespoons of the liquid, discard the woody stems and finely chop the caps.

3 **In a separate bowl** combine the soy sauce, hoisin sauce, rice wine, reserved mushroom liquid, sugar, sesame oil and cornflour mixture.

4 **Heat a wok** over high heat. Add the oil and swirl to coat. Cook the spring onion, garlic, ginger and coriander stems for 1 minute. Add the tofu and cook for 1 minute. Add the mushrooms, cabbage and water chestnuts and cook for 2–3 minutes, or until the cabbage has wilted.

5 **Pour in the** combined soy sauce mixture and cook for 1 minute. Add the coriander leaves and toss to combine.

6 **To serve,** divide the mixture among the lettuce cups, garnish with the spring onion and drizzle with hoisin sauce.

SHIITAKE MUSHROOMS WITH NAM PRIK SAUCE

SERVES 4

BATTER

25 g (4½ oz/1 cup) plain (all-purpose) flour

1 teaspoon salt

3 tablespoons coconut milk

250 ml (9 fl oz/1 cup) ice-cold water

vegetable oil, for deep-frying

200 g (7 oz) small–medium fresh shiitake mushrooms

NAM PRIK SAUCE

1 tablespoon soy sauce

2 tablespoons lemon juice

2 teaspoons sugar

2 green chillies, halved lengthways, seeded (see Note)

2 red chillies, halved lengthways, seeded

3 garlic cloves, halved

3 red Asian shallots, halved

2 tomatoes, cut into 2 cm (¾ inch) slices

1 small eggplant (aubergine) (about 150 g/5½ oz), cut into 2 cm (¾ inch) slices

1 To make the batter, combine the flour, salt, coconut milk and cold water in a bowl. Don't beat it too much — it can still have a few lumps. If it seems too thick, add a little more cold water. Leave for 30 minutes while making the nam prik sauce.

2 To make the sauce, preheat the grill (broiler) to high. Put the soy sauce, lemon juice and sugar in a small saucepan and heat gently for 1–2 minutes to dissolve the sugar. Remove from the heat. Wrap the chillies, garlic and shallots in a foil package and wrap the tomatoes and eggplant in a separate foil package. Put both packages under the grill for 10–15 minutes, or until the spices and vegetables begin to soften. Remove from the foil and peel the skin from the eggplant, tomatoes and chillies. Pound all the ingredients together in a mortar and pestle or small food processor. Transfer to a bowl and stir in the sauce mixture, mixing well. Spoon into a serving dish and set aside.

3 Half fill a wok with oil and heat to 180°C (350°F), or until a cube of bread dropped in the oil browns in 15 seconds. Working in batches, dip the mushrooms in the batter, allowing any excess batter to drip off, and cook for 1½–2 minutes, or until crisp and golden. Take care not to overcrowd the oil. Drain on crumpled paper towels. Serve immediately with the nam prik sauce.

Note: If you like your sauces really hot, leave a few of the seeds in the chillies.

CHARGRILLED VEGETABLE SKEWERS WITH HARISSA

MAKES 8 SKEWERS

HARISSA

2 teaspoons cumin seeds

½ teaspoon caraway seeds

75 g (2½ oz) large red chillies, chopped

3 garlic cloves, chopped

1 teaspoon sea salt flakes

50 g (1¾ oz) tomato paste
(concentrated purée)

4 tablespoons olive oil

1 eggplant (aubergine), cut into 2 cm
(¾ inch) cubes

150 g (5½ oz) button mushrooms,
stems trimmed and sliced in half

250 g (9 oz) cherry tomatoes

1 zucchini (courgette), sliced

125 g (4½ oz/½ cup) Greek-style
yoghurt

steamed rice and coriander (cilantro)
leaves, to serve

1 Soak eight bamboo skewers in water for 20 minutes. Heat a small non-stick frying pan over a medium–high heat and dry-fry the cumin and caraway seeds for 30 seconds, or until fragrant.

2 Place in the bowl of a small food processor with the chillies, garlic, salt, 50 ml (1¾ fl oz) of water and tomato paste. Purée until almost smooth. Gradually add the olive oil and purée until combined.

3 Preheat a barbecue or chargrill plate to medium–high heat. Thread the eggplant, mushrooms, tomatoes and zucchini onto the skewers. Brush generously with half the harissa.

4 Cook the skewers for 5–7 minutes on each side, or until golden.

5 Serve the skewers with the extra harissa, the yoghurt and the steamed rice. Garnish with coriander, if desired.

MUSHROOM MELTS

SERVES 6

1 large red capsicum (pepper)

6 field mushrooms (about 7 cm/
  2¾ inches in diameter)

60 g (2¼ oz/¼ cup) ready-made pesto

60 g (2¼ oz/½ cup) grated
  cheddar cheese

6 slices sourdough or woodfired bread

2–3 tablespoons extra virgin olive oil

2–3 garlic cloves, peeled and cut in half

chives, to serve (optional)

1 Heat the grill (broiler) to high. Cut the capsicum into large flat pieces, discarding the seeds and membrane. Arrange skin side up on the grill tray and grill until the skin blackens and blisters. Leave to cool in a plastic bag, then peel away the skin and roughly chop the flesh. Turn the grill down to medium.

2 Arrange the mushrooms gill side up on the grill tray and spread with the pesto. Sprinkle with the capsicum and cheddar and season with freshly ground black pepper. Grill for 3–5 minutes, or until the cheese has melted and turned a light golden brown — you may need to grill the mushrooms in two batches. When you're done, remove the mushrooms from the heat and leave to cool slightly.

3 Put the bread slices on the grill tray and toast lightly on both sides. Lightly drizzle both sides of the bread with the oil, then gently rub all over with a cut garlic clove. Sit the mushrooms on the toasts. Serve at once, topped with chives.

VEGETABLE PAKORAS WITH CORIANDER CHUTNEY

SERVES 4

650 g (1 lb 7 oz) selection of vegetables such as zucchini (courgette), red capsicum (pepper), orange sweet potato and onion (about 500 g/ 1 lb 2 oz peeled weight in total)

CHICKPEA BATTER

125 g (4½ oz/heaped 1 cup) besan (chickpea flour)

1 teaspoon salt

2 teaspoons curry powder

1 teaspoon ground turmeric

1 tablespoon sunflower oil

1 tablespoon lemon juice

CORIANDER CHUTNEY

4 large handfuls coriander (cilantro) leaves

1 large green chilli, deseeded and finely chopped

1 garlic clove, crushed

250 g (9 oz/1 cup) Greek-style yoghurt

1 tablespoon lemon juice

vegetable oil, for deep-frying

1 Peel and cut the vegetables into thin strips.

2 Sift the besan into a bowl and stir in the salt, curry powder and turmeric. Make a well in the centre and gradually beat in the oil, lemon juice and 185 ml (6 fl oz/¾ cup) of water to make a smooth batter with the consistency of thick cream.

3 To make the chutney, put the coriander, chilli and garlic in a food processor with 2 tablespoons of cold water and process until smooth. Transfer to a bowl and stir in the yoghurt and lemon juice. Season to taste and set aside.

4 Heat about 5 cm (2 inches) of vegetable oil in a wok or deep saucepan to 180°C (350°F), or until a cube of bread dropped in the oil browns in 15 seconds. Lightly whisk the batter and stir in the vegetables. Carefully slip bundles of batter-coated vegetables into the hot oil and fry in batches for 2–3 minutes, or until golden. Drain on paper towel and keep warm in the oven while cooking the remaining vegetables.

5 Serve the pakoras with the coriander chutney.

SPRING ROLLS

MAKES 24

5 dried shiitake mushrooms

50 g (1¾ oz) dried bean vermicelli
  noodles

2 tablespoons peanut oil

2 garlic cloves, chopped

1 large carrot, cut into 5 cm (2 inch)
  matchsticks

90 g (3¼ oz/1 cup) bean sprouts,
  tails trimmed

2 spring onions (scallions), sliced
  on the diagonal

1½ tablespoons oyster sauce

2 teaspoons soy sauce

1 teaspoon sugar

PASTE

1 tablespoon cornflour (cornstarch)

2 tablespoons of boiling water

24 mini spring roll wrappers
  (12.5 x 12.5 cm/5 x 5 inches)

oil, for deep-frying

your choice of dipping sauce, to serve
  (see recipes on pages 156/157)

1 Soak the shiitake mushrooms in hot water for about 10 minutes. Drain. Discard the woody stems and thinly slice the caps.

2 In a separate bowl, soak the noodles in warm water for 10 minutes. Drain and cut into shorter segments.

3 Heat the peanut oil in a wok over medium heat, add the garlic and toss until aromatic. Add the carrot and stir-fry for 1–2 minutes. Add the noodles, shiitake mushrooms, bean sprouts and spring onion, toss for another minute, then stir in the oyster sauce, soy sauce and sugar. Remove from the heat and allow to cool.

4 Make a paste by adding the boiling water to the cornflour. Mix well.

5 Put one spring roll wrapper on a board with a corner pointing towards you. Put 1 tablespoon of filling in the centre and firmly roll, tucking in the sides. As you near the final corner, dab with a little of the cornflour paste to enclose the filling. Repeat to make 24 spring rolls. Cover the remaining wrappers and completed spring rolls with a damp tea towel (dish towel) to prevent them drying out.

6 Fill a wok one-third full of oil and heat to 190°C (375°F), or until a cube of bread dropped in the oil browns in 10 seconds. Add the spring rolls in batches and cook for 30–60 seconds, or until crisp and golden brown. Drain on crumpled paper towels.

7 Serve hot with your choice of dipping sauce (see recipes on pages 156/157).

SPICY CORN PUFFS

MAKES 36

2 corn cobs

3 tablespoons chopped fresh coriander
    (cilantro) leaves

6 spring onions, finely chopped

1 small red chilli, seeded and finely
    chopped

1 large egg

2 teaspoons ground cumin

½ teaspoon ground coriander (cilantro)

125 g (4 oz/1 cup) plain flour

oil, for deep-frying

sweet chilli sauce, to serve

1   **Cut down the side** of the corn with a sharp knife to
release the kernels. Roughly chop the kernels, then place them
in a large bowl. Holding the cobs over the bowl, scrape down
the sides of the cobs with a knife to release any corn juice
from the cob into the bowl.

2   **Add the fresh coriander,** spring onion, chilli, egg, cumin,
ground coriander, 1 teaspoon salt and some freshly ground
black pepper to the bowl and stir well.

3   **Add the flour** and mix well. The texture of the batter will
vary depending on the juiciness of the corn. If the mixture is
too dry, add 1 tablespoon water, but no more than that as the
batter should be quite dry. Stand for 10 minutes.

4   **Fill a large** heavy-based saucepan or deep-fryer one-third
full of oil and heat to 180°C (350°F), or until a cube of bread
dropped in the oil browns in 15 seconds. Drop slightly heaped
teaspoons of the corn batter into the oil and cook for about
1½ minutes, or until puffed and golden. Drain on crumpled
paper towels.

5   **Serve hot** with your choice of dipping sauce (see recipes
on pages 156/157).

UDON NOODLE SUSHI ROLLS

MAKES 36 PIECES

300 g (10½ oz) flat udon or soba
   noodles

6 roasted nori sheets

50 g (1¾ oz) pickled daikon, cut into
   thin strips

3 tablespoons drained pickled ginger,
   sliced

light soy sauce, to serve

1 **Cook the noodles** according to the packet instructions until *al dente*. Rinse under cold water and pat dry.

2 **Working on a flat surface,** place one sheet of nori on a sushi mat. Arrange one sixth of the noodles along the bottom half of the nori sheet, then arrange one-sixth of the daikon and pickled ginger along the centre of the noodles.

3 **Roll the nori up** firmly to enclose the filling. Cut the roll in half across the middle, then cut each half into three equal pieces. Repeat with the remaining ingredients.

4 **Serve** with a little bowl of light soy sauce for dipping.

BARBECUED CORN CAKES

MAKES 12

125 g (4½ oz/1 cup) plain (all-purpose)
   flour

75 g (2½ oz/½ cup) fine polenta

1 teaspoon baking powder

1 teaspoon salt

1 egg

170 ml (5½ oz/⅔ cup) buttermilk

1 cooked corn cob, kernels cut off

1 tablespoon chopped pickled
   jalapeño chilli

1 large red chilli, seeded and chopped

1 tablespoon chopped coriander
   (cilantro) leaves

1 tablespoon chopped parsley

olive oil, for brushing

TOMATO AND AVOCADO RELISH

4 Roma (plum) tomatoes, quartered

1 tablespoon lime juice

1 avocado, cut into 2 cm (¾ inch) cubes

1 **Preheat a barbecue grill plate** or flat plate to medium.
Put the flour, polenta, baking powder and salt in a large bowl,
making a well in the centre. In a small bowl, whisk together
the egg and buttermilk, then pour into the flour mixture and
stir to thoroughly combine. Mix through the corn, chillies,
coriander and parsley.

2 **Brush the barbecue hotplate** with 1 tablespoon of oil.
Cook the tomato quarters for 2 minutes on each side, then
remove and allow to cool.

3 **To make the tomato and avocado relish,** roughly chop
the cooled tomato and place in a bowl with the lime juice
and ½ teaspoon salt. Add the avocado cubes, mix gently and
set aside.

4 **Brush the hotplate** with another tablespoon of oil. Spoon
2 tablespoons of corn cake batter onto the hotplate to form a
round cake. Repeat until the batter is used up. You should have
enough batter to make 12 corn cakes. Cook for 2 minutes, or
until bubbles appear on the surface. Turn and cook for a further
2–3 minutes, or until golden brown, brushing the hotplate with
more oil if necessary.

5 **Serve** the corn cakes hot, with the tomato and avocado
relish on the side.

ZUCCHINI, PROVOLONE AND CAPSICUM BRUSCHETTA

SERVES 4

2 small yellow capsicums (peppers)

2 zucchini (courgettes)

oil, for brushing

3 tablespoons torn purple basil leaves

50 g (1¾ oz) shaved or very thinly sliced provolone cheese

1 garlic clove, crushed

1½ tablespoons extra virgin olive oil

4 x 2.5 cm (1 inch) thick slices ciabatta or other Italian-style bread

2 garlic cloves, halved

1 **Preheat a barbecue grill plate** to medium. Cut each capsicum into four flat pieces and remove the seeds and membranes. Place skin side down on the hotplate and grill for about 8 minutes, or until the skins blacken and blister. Leave to cool in a plastic bag for about 5 minutes, then peel away the skin, slice the flesh into two long strips and put them in a bowl.

2 **Slice the zucchini lengthways** into 5 mm (¼ inch) ribbons and brush both sides with oil. Put them on the hotplate and sprinkle lightly with salt. Cook for 2–3 minutes on each side, or until the slices turn soft and light brown grill lines form on both sides. Add to the capsicum strips along with the basil.

3 **Slice the provolone into similar-sized strips** as the capsicum and add them to the grilled vegetables. Combine the crushed garlic and extra virgin olive oil and season to taste. Drizzle over the grilled vegetables and toss lightly.

4 **Put the ciabatta slices** on a clean section of the barbecue and cook for 1 minute, or until grill lines form. Rotate the slices at right angles and grill for another minute to give a crisscross chargrill pattern underneath. Turn the slices over and repeat on the other side.

5 **Rub half a cut garlic clove** over both sides of each slice of toasted bread. Transfer to a serving plate and top with a pile of the grilled vegetables. Serve warm or at room temperature.

DEEP-FRIED BEAN CURD ROLLS

MAKES 8

FILLING

10 dried shiitake mushrooms

2 tablespoons vegetable or peanut oil

1 carrot, cut into thin matchsticks

2 garlic cloves, chopped

100 g (3½ oz) snowpeas (mangetout),
    topped and tailed and thinly sliced on
    the diagonal

2 tablespoons oyster sauce

2 teaspoons soy sauce

1 teaspoon sugar

1 teaspoon sesame oil

200 g (7 oz) dried bean curd sheets

PASTE

1 tablespoon cornflour (cornstarch)

2½ tablespoons water

vegetable oil, for deep-frying

your choice of dipping sauce, to serve
    (see recipes on pages 156/157)

1   **To make the filling,** soak the shiitake mushrooms in hot water for 10 minutes. Drain. Discard the woody stems and slice the caps.

2   **Heat the oil in a wok** over medium–high heat and stir-fry the carrot for 1 minute, or until softened slightly. Add the garlic, mushrooms and snowpeas, then stir in the oyster sauce, soy sauce, sugar and sesame oil until heated through. Remove from the heat. Cool to room temperature.

3   **Trim the bean curd sheets** to eight rectangles about 15 x 20 cm (6 x 8 inches), put them on a large tray and cover with cold water. Leave to soak for a few minutes, until softened, then remove carefully from the water and put on a clean dry tea towel (dish towel). Pat dry slightly. Divide the filling into eight portions.

4   **Mix cornflour** with the water to form a paste Take one bean curd wrapper and put a portion of filling in the centre. Roll up firmly, folding in the ends. Dab cornflour paste on the ends to enclose. Repeat with the remaining sheets and filling.

5   **Half-fill a wok** with oil and heat to 190°C (375°F), or until a cube of bread dropped in the oil browns in 10 seconds. Add the rolls a few at a time and deep-fry for 3–4 minutes, or until golden and crisp, turning over halfway through.

6   **Serve hot,** either whole or sliced in half on the diagonal, with dipping sauce (see recipes on pages 156/157).

Note: Bean curd sheets are very delicate and need care and patience to work with. You may want to buy an extra packet as some may break or tear.

OPEN VEGETABLE DUMPLINGS

8 dried shiitake mushrooms

3 garlic cloves, crushed

2 teaspoons grated fresh ginger

5 spring onions (scallions),
  finely chopped

60 g (2¼ oz/¼ bunch) water spinach
  (ong choy) or baby spinach, chopped

60 g (2¼ oz/⅓ cup) diced water
  chestnuts

40 g (1½ oz/¼ cup) toasted unsalted
  peanuts, chopped

3 tablespoons chopped coriander
  (cilantro) leaves and stems

2 teaspoons Chinese rice wine

2 tablespoons kecap manis

1 teaspoon sesame oil

15 round won ton wrappers

4 tablespoons sweet plum sauce,
  to serve

1 Soak the shiitake mushrooms in boiling water for 5 minutes, or until softened. Drain, discard the woody stems and finely chop the caps. Transfer to a bowl with the garlic, ginger, spring onion, water spinach, water chestnuts, peanuts, coriander, rice wine, kecap manis and sesame oil and stir until well combined.

2 Put 1 tablespoon of the mixture in the centre of a won ton wrapper, and lightly brush the edges with water. Bring the edges up around the filling, pleating as you go to encase the filling. The top should be open. Repeat with the remaining wrappers and filling to make 15 dumplings.

3 Line a large 30 cm (12 inch) bamboo steamer with baking paper and punch with holes. Arrange the dumplings on top in a single layer. Sit the steamer over a wok of simmering water and steam, covered, for 5 minutes, or until cooked through. If you don't have a large steamer, cook the dumplings in batches or use two smaller steamers, swapping them halfway through. Serve with plum sauce.

Note: The sweet plum sauce comes in a similar bottle to sweet chilli sauce and is fairly light in colour. It is not the same as plum sauce sold in western-style supermarkets. Look for it in Asian food shops.

CARROT TIMBALES WITH SAFFRON AND LEEK SAUCE

SERVES 6

60 g (2¼ oz) butter

2 leeks, white part only, sliced

2 garlic cloves, crushed

1 kg (2 lb 4 oz) carrots, sliced

375 ml (13 fl oz/1½ cups) vegetable stock

1½ tablespoons finely chopped sage

60 ml (2 fl oz/¼ cup) pouring cream

4 eggs, lightly beaten

SAFFRON AND LEEK SAUCE

40 g (1½ oz) butter

1 small leek, white part only, finely sliced

1 large garlic clove, crushed

60 ml (2 fl oz/¼ cup) white wine

a pinch of saffron threads

90 g (3¼ oz/⅓ cup) crème fraîche or light sour cream

1 **Preheat the oven** to 170°C (325°F/Gas 3). Lightly grease six 185 ml (6 fl oz/¾ cup) timbale moulds or ramekins.

2 **Melt the butter** in a saucepan and sauté the leek over medium heat for 3–4 minutes. Add the garlic and carrot and cook for 2–3 minutes. Pour in the stock and 500 ml (17 fl oz /2 cups) water. Bring to the boil, then reduce the heat, cover and simmer for 5 minutes, or until the carrot is tender. Strain, reserving 185 ml (6 fl oz/¾ cup) of the liquid.

3 **Blend the carrot,** sage and 125 ml (4 fl oz/½ cup) of the reserved liquid until smooth. Cool slightly. Stir in the cream and egg, season and pour into the moulds. Place the moulds in a roasting tin and pour in enough hot water to come halfway up the side. Bake for 30–40 minutes, or until just set.

4 **To make the sauce,** melt the butter in a saucepan and sauté the leek over medium heat for 3–4 minutes without browning. Add the garlic and cook for 30 seconds. Add the wine, remaining reserved liquid and saffron, then simmer for 5 minutes, or until reduced. Stir in the crème fraîche.

5 **Invert the timbales** onto serving plates and serve with the saffron and leek sauce.

FALAFEL WITH TAHINI YOGHURT DRESSING

SERVES 4

FALAFEL
250 g (9 oz) dried chickpeas

1 onion, finely chopped

2 garlic cloves, crushed

5 large handfuls parsley

4 large handfuls coriander (cilantro) leaves

2 teaspoons ground coriander

1 teaspoon ground cumin

½ teaspoon baking powder

TAHINI YOGHURT DRESSING
3 tablespoons Greek-style yoghurt

1 tablespoon tahini paste

1 garlic clove, crushed

1 tablespoon lemon juice

3 tablespoons extra virgin olive oil

vegetable oil, for frying

125 g (4½ oz) rocket (arugula) leaves, to serve

1 Put the dried chickpeas into a bowl and add enough cold water to cover them by about 12 cm (4½ inches) and leave to soak overnight.

2 Drain the chickpeas well and transfer to a food processor. Process until coarsely ground. Add the remaining falafel ingredients and process until smooth and a vibrant green colour. Leave to infuse for 30 minutes.

3 To make the tahini dressing, put all the ingredients in a bowl and whisk together until smooth. Season to taste and set aside until required.

4 Using slightly wet hands, shape the falafel mixture into 24 ovals (about the size of an egg). Heat 5 cm (2 inches) vegetable oil in a wok or deep saucepan and fry the falafel in batches for 2–3 minutes, or until dark brown. Drain on paper towel and keep warm in a low oven while cooking the remaining mixture.

5 Arrange the rocket leaves on serving plates, top with the falafel and drizzle over the tahini dressing. Serve immediately.

POTS OF BAKED RICOTTA AND MUSHROOMS

SERVES 4

20 g (¾ oz) butter

1 teaspoon olive oil

125 g (4½ oz/1⅓ cups) sliced button
   mushrooms

1 garlic clove, crushed

1 teaspoon chopped marjoram, plus
   4 marjoram sprigs

pinch of ground nutmeg

extra virgin olive oil, for drizzling

400 g (14 oz) block of ricotta cheese
   (see Note)

1 **Preheat the oven** to 180°C (350°F/Gas 4).

2 **Heat the butter** and olive oil in a small frying pan.
Add the mushrooms and garlic and briefly fry over high heat
until lightly golden.

3 **Remove from the heat,** then stir in the marjoram, nutmeg,
and some sea salt and freshly ground black pepper to taste.

4 **Brush four 125 ml** (4 fl oz/1/2 cup) ramekins with a little
extra virgin olive oil and line the bases with a circle of baking
paper. Put the tip of a marjoram sprig in the base of each
ramekin.

5 **Gently mix together** the mushroom mixture and ricotta
cheese. Divide among the ramekins and press down firmly.

6 **Bake for** 20–25 minutes, or until the tops are crusty and
the mixture has started to shrink from the side of the ramekins.
Remove from the oven and leave to cool for 5 minutes before
turning out.

7 **Serve** hot, warm or cold, drizzled with a little extra virgin
olive oil.

Note: Buy the ricotta for this recipe from a bulk block; it
is much drier and has a better texture than the type sold
in pre-weighed tubs. Blocks of ricotta can be found in the
delicatessen section of larger supermarkets.

VEGETABLE TEMPURA WITH WASABI SOY

SERVES 4

WASABI SOY
4 tablespoons salt-reduced soy sauce

2 teaspoons wasabi paste

TEMPURA BATTER
150 g (5½ oz/1¼ cups) plain
(all-purpose) flour

60 g (2¼ oz/½ cup) cornflour
(cornstarch)

2 eggs

vegetable oil, for deep-frying

200 g (7 oz) orange sweet potato, cut
into 1 cm (½ inch) thick slices

200 g (7 oz) carrots, cut into thick sticks

175 g (6 oz/1 bunch) asparagus,
trimmed, cut into 4–5 cm
(1½ –2 inch) pieces

100 g (3½ oz) green beans or snow
peas (mangetout), trimmed

1 red capsicum (pepper), cut into large
chunks

1 **To make the wasabi soy,** put the soy sauce and wasabi in a small bowl. Mix until well combined, then set aside.

2 **To make the tempura batter,** put the flour, cornflour and a pinch of salt in a large bowl. Mix well to combine. Whisk 250 ml (9 fl oz/1 cup) iced water and the eggs together. Add to the flour mixture and mix until just combined. Do not overmix, it doesn't matter if there are lumps in the batter.

3 **Preheat the oven** to 200°C (400°F/Gas 6). Line a large baking tray with paper towel. Heat the oil in a large wide-based saucepan over medium–high heat until it reaches 180°C (350°F), or until a cube of bread dropped in the oil browns in 15 seconds.

4 **Dip the sweet potato** into the batter, carefully shaking off any excess. Add to the oil and cook for 3–4 minutes, or until the batter is crisp and light golden. Use a slotted spoon to transfer to the paper towel. Once drained, transfer to the baking tray. Place in the oven to keep warm and crisp while repeating with the carrots, asparagus, beans and capsicum. Serve the vegetable tempura immediately with wasabi soy mixture.

SOUPS

VEGETABLE LAKSA

SERVES 4

250 g (9 oz) dried rice vermicelli

1 tablespoon vegetable oil

3 tablespoons laksa paste

750 ml (26 fl oz/3 cups) coconut milk

750 ml (26 fl oz/3 cups) good-quality
vegetable stock

90 g (3¼ oz/½ cup) baby corn, halved
diagonally

2 snake (yard-long) beans, cut into
4 cm (1½ inch) lengths

¼ Chinese cabbage (wong bok),
shredded

4 fried tofu puffs, halved

150 g (5½ oz/1⅔ cups) bean sprouts,
tails trimmed

1 Lebanese (short) cucumber, cut into
matchsticks

3 tablespoons coarsely chopped
Vietnamese mint

1 small red chilli, thinly sliced

1 Put the vermicelli in a bowl and cover with boiling water.

2 Heat the oil in a large wok over medium heat and cook the laksa paste for 1–2 minutes, or until fragrant. Stir in the coconut milk and stock and bring to the boil.

3 Add the baby corn and snake beans and simmer for about 3 minutes. Stir in the cabbage.

4 Drain the vermicelli, rinse under hot water and drain again. Spoon into four deep serving bowls.

5 Divide the tofu puffs, bean sprouts and cucumber among the bowls.

6 Ladle the vegetables and broth into the bowls and scatter the mint leaves and chilli over the top. Serve immediately.

Note: The soup should be eaten within 1 day. It is not suitable for freezing.

GREAT TASTES VEGETARIAN

ROASTED LEEK AND CELERIAC SOUP

SERVES 4

2 tablespoons olive oil

800 g (1 lb 12 oz/about 2 large) leeks, white part only, cut into 5 cm (2 inch) lengths

1 garlic bulb, unpeeled, halved

800 g (1 lb 12 oz/1 medium) celeriac, chopped

250 ml (9 fl oz/1 cup) milk

125 ml (4 fl oz/½ cup) thick (double/ heavy) cream

2 tablespoons snipped chives

slices of toasted baguette, to serve

1   Preheat the oven to 200°C (400°F/Gas 6). Put the olive oil in a roasting tin and heat in the oven for 5 minutes. Add the leek and garlic bulb halves and season with salt and freshly ground black pepper. Shake the roasting tin to coat the vegetables with the oil. Roast for 20–25 minutes, or until the leek is tender. Remove the leek and roast the garlic for a further 10–15 minutes, or until tender when pierced with the tip of a knife.

2   Meanwhile, put the celeriac and 750 ml (26 fl oz/3 cups) of water in a large saucepan. Cover and bring to the boil, then reduce the heat to medium–low and simmer for 20 minutes, or until tender. Add the roasted leek.

3   Squeeze or scoop the garlic into the saucepan. Season with salt and freshly ground black pepper and mix well. Add the milk.

4   Remove the saucepan from the heat. Using an immersion blender fitted with the chopping blade, whizz for 45 seconds, or until puréed. Stir through the cream and gently reheat the soup. Check the seasoning and thickness, adding additional milk if the soup is too thick. Sprinkle with the chives. Serve topped with slices of toasted baguette.

Note: The soup will keep in the refrigerator, covered, for up to 4 days, or in an airtight container in the freezer for up to 1 month.

SPICED PUMPKIN AND LENTIL SOUP

SERVES 4

1 kg (2 lb 4 oz) pumpkin (squash)

2 tablespoons olive oil

1 large onion, chopped

3 garlic cloves, chopped

1 teaspoon ground turmeric

½ teaspoon ground coriander

½ teaspoon ground cumin

½ teaspoon chilli flakes

135 g (4¾ oz/½ cup) red lentils, rinsed
and drained

1 litre (35 fl oz/4 cups) boiling water

90 g (3¼ oz/⅓ cup) plain yoghurt,
to serve

slices of toasted crusty bread, to serve

1 Peel, seed and cube the pumpkin to give 700 g
(1 lb 9 oz/4½ cups) of flesh.

2 Heat the oil in a large saucepan over medium heat.
Add the onion and garlic and fry for 5 minutes, or until
softened, being careful not to burn the garlic.

3 Add the turmeric, coriander, cumin and chilli flakes and
fry, stirring constantly, for 2 minutes.

4 Add the pumpkin, red lentils and boiling water. Bring
to the boil, then reduce the heat and simmer, covered, for
20 minutes, or until the pumpkin and lentils are tender.
Set aside to cool for 5 minutes.

5 Using an immersion blender fitted with the chopping
blade, whizz the soup for 25–35 seconds, or until evenly
chopped. Season well with salt and freshly ground black
pepper and reheat the soup.

6 To serve, ladle the soup into four bowls, top with a
spoonful of the yoghurt and sprinkle with freshly ground
black pepper.

Note: The soup will keep in the refrigerator, covered, for
up to 6 days, or in an airtight container in the freezer for up to
1 month.

WATERCRESS, LEEK AND POTATO SOUP

SERVES 4

350 g (12 oz) watercress, trimmed

1 tablespoon oil

1 leek, white part only, chopped

2 garlic cloves, chopped

1 celery stalk, chopped

1 teaspoon freshly grated nutmeg

500 g (1 lb 2 oz/4 medium) potatoes, chopped

1 litre (35 fl oz/4 cups) vegetable stock

250 ml (9 fl oz/1 cup) milk

1 handful mint

1 **Reserve** a few watercress leaves for serving. Pick off the remaining leaves in bunches, discarding the thick stems. Roughly chop and reserve the watercress.

2 **Heat the oil** in a large heavy-based saucepan. Add the leek, garlic and celery. Stir for 2 minutes to coat the vegetables in the oil. Reduce the heat, cover and simmer, stirring occasionally, for 5 minutes. Do not allow the vegetables to brown.

3 **Add the nutmeg**, potato and stock. Slowly bring to the boil, then reduce the heat and simmer, covered, for 20 minutes. Stir in the chopped watercress. Set aside to cool for 10 minutes.

4 **Stir the milk** and mint into the soup. Using an immersion blender fitted with the chopping blade, whizz for 1 minute, or until puréed to the desired consistency.

5 **Gently reheat the soup** and season well with salt and freshly ground black pepper.

6 **To serve**, ladle into bowls and garnish with the reserved watercress leaves.

Note: The soup will keep in the refrigerator, covered, for up to 4 days, or in an airtight container in the freezer for up to 1 month.

ZUCCHINI AND BASIL SOUP

SERVES 4

1 large onion, finely chopped

3 garlic cloves, very finely chopped

½ teaspoon coriander seeds

2 celery stalks, finely diced

6 zucchini (courgettes), roughly diced

3 large waxy potatoes, diced

1.25 litres (44 fl oz/5 cups) vegetable stock

125 g (4½ oz/½ cup) crème fraîche or sour cream

1 large handful basil, torn

2 tablespoons finely chopped flat-leaf (Italian) parsley

sea salt, to serve

slices of toasted crusty bread, to serve

1 Put the onion, garlic, coriander seeds, celery, zucchini, potato and stock in a large heavy-based saucepan. Bring to the boil over medium heat. Partially cover the saucepan and gently simmer for 12–15 minutes, or until all the vegetables are cooked through.

2 Meanwhile, put the crème fraîche or sour cream in a small bowl with half the basil and the parsley. Mix together using a fork, then set aside.

3 Remove the saucepan from the heat. Using an immersion blender fitted with the chopping blade, whizz the soup for 20 seconds, or until it is semi-smooth.

4 Stir in the remaining basil. Season with salt and freshly ground black pepper, to taste.

5 Divide the crème fraîche mixture among four bowls, ladle the soup into the bowls and sprinkle with sea salt and freshly ground black pepper. Serve immediately.

Note: The soup will keep in the refrigerator, covered, for up to 4 days, or in an airtight container in the freezer for up to 1 month.

CREAMY BRUSSELS SPROUT AND LEEK SOUP

SERVES 4

1 tablespoon olive oil

2 garlic cloves, chopped

3 leeks, white part only, sliced

300 g (10½ oz) brussels sprouts,
  roughly chopped

750 ml (26 fl oz/3 cups) vegetable stock

185 ml (6 fl oz/¾ cup) pouring cream
  or milk

slices of toasted crusty bread, to serve

1 Heat the oil in a large saucepan over medium heat. Add the garlic and leek, cover and fry, stirring often, for 5 minutes.

2 Add the brussels sprouts, stir to combine, cover and cook, stirring often, for 5 minutes.

3 Add the stock and season with salt and freshly ground black pepper. Bring to the boil, then reduce the heat, cover the pan and simmer for 10 minutes, or until the vegetables are very tender. Set aside to cool for 10 minutes.

4 Using an immersion blender fitted with the chopping blade, whizz the soup for 25–30 seconds, or until puréed. Stir through the cream or milk and gently reheat the soup.

5 Serve with slices of toasted crusty bread.

Note: The soup will keep in the refrigerator, covered, for up to 4 days, or in an airtight container in the freezer for up to 1 month.

BARLEY SOUP WITH GOLDEN PARSNIPS

SERVES 6

200 g (6½ oz) pearl barley

1 tablespoon oil

2 onions, chopped

2 cloves garlic, finely chopped

2 carrots, chopped

2 potatoes, chopped

2 celery sticks, chopped

2 bay leaves, torn in half

2 litres chicken stock

125 ml (4 fl oz/ ½ cup) milk

40 g (1¼ oz) butter

3 parsnips, cubed

1 teaspoon soft brown sugar

chopped fresh parsley, to serve

1 Soak the barley in water overnight. Drain. Place in a saucepan with 2 litres water. Bring to the boil, then reduce the heat and simmer, partially covered, for 1¼ hours, or until tender. Drain the barley.

2 Heat the oil in a large saucepan, add the onion, garlic, carrot, potato and celery, and cook for 3 minutes. Stir well and cook, covered, for 15 minutes over low heat, stirring occasionally.

3 Add the barley, bay leaves, stock, milk, 2 teaspoons of salt and 1 teaspoon of freshly ground black pepper. Bring to the boil, then reduce the heat and simmer the soup, partially covered, for 35 minutes. If the soup is too thick, add about 1 cup (250 ml/8 fl oz) cold water, a little at a time, until the soup reaches your preferred consistency.

4 While the soup is simmering, melt the butter in a frying pan, add the parsnip and toss in the butter. Sprinkle with the sugar and cook until golden brown and tender.

5 Serve the parsnip on top of the soup and sprinkle with the parsley.

Note: The soup will keep in the refrigerator, covered, for up to 4 days, or in an airtight container in the freezer for up to 1 month.

ALSACE MUSHROOM SOUP

SERVES 4

10 g (¼ oz) dried porcini mushrooms

250 ml (9 fl oz/1 cup) hot water

50 g (1¾ oz) butter

1 onion, roughly chopped

4 French shallots, chopped

1 large potato, about 185 g (6½ oz), chopped

1 celery stalk, chopped

2 garlic cloves, chopped

1 small red chilli, seeded and chopped

175 g (6 oz) flat mushrooms, roughly chopped

175 g (6 oz) Swiss brown mushrooms, roughly chopped

750 ml (26 fl oz/3 cups) vegetable stock

2 large thyme sprigs

1–2 teaspoons lemon juice, to taste

90 g (3¼ oz/⅓ cup) sour cream, to serve

2 tablespoons finely chopped flat-leaf (Italian) parsley, to serve

1 tablespoon grated lemon zest, to serve

slices of toasted crusty bread, to serve

1 Put the porcini mushrooms in a small bowl and pour over the hot water. Set aside to soften for 10 minutes.

2 Meanwhile, heat the butter in a large heavy-based saucepan. Add the onion, shallots, potato, celery, garlic and chilli. Stir for 2 minutes to coat the vegetables in the butter. Reduce the heat, cover and simmer, stirring occasionally, for 5 minutes. Do not allow the vegetables to brown.

3 Add the fresh mushrooms to the saucepan and cook, stirring, for 2–3 minutes. Add the stock, thyme sprigs and porcini mushrooms with their soaking water. Slowly bring to the boil over low heat, then reduce the heat and simmer, covered, for 15 minutes. Discard the thyme sprigs. Set aside to cool slightly.

4 Using an immersion blender fitted with the chopping blade, whizz the soup for 15–20 seconds, or until roughly puréed. The soup should still have texture. Add the lemon juice, to taste, and season well with salt and freshly ground black pepper.

5 Gently reheat the soup and ladle into warm bowls. Top with a spoonful of the sour cream and sprinkle with the parsley and lemon zest.

6 Serve with slices of toasted crusty bread.

Note: The soup will keep in the refrigerator, covered, for up to 4 days, or in an airtight container in the freezer for up to 1 month.

CHICKPEA AND HERB DUMPLING SOUP

SERVES 4

1 tablespoon oil

1 onion, chopped

2 cloves garlic, crushed

2 teaspoons ground cumin

1 teaspoon ground coriander (cilantro)

¼ teaspoon chilli powder

2 x 300 g (10 oz) cans chickpeas, drained

875 ml (28 fl oz/3½ cups) vegetable stock

2 x 425 g (14 oz) cans chopped tomatoes

1 tablespoon chopped fresh coriander (cilantro) leaves

125 g (4 oz/1 cup) self-raising flour

25 g (1 oz) butter, chopped

2 tablespoons grated fresh Parmesan

2 tablespoons mixed chopped fresh herbs (chives, flat-leaf parsley and coriander leaves)

60 ml (2 fl oz/¼ cup) milk

1 Heat the oil in a large saucepan and cook the onion over medium heat for 2–3 minutes, or until soft. Add the garlic, cumin, ground coriander and chilli, and cook for 1 minute, or until fragrant.

2 Add the chickpeas, stock and tomato. Bring to the boil, then reduce the heat and simmer, covered, for 10 minutes. Stir in the coriander.

3 To make the dumplings, sift the flour into a bowl and add the chopped butter. Rub the butter into the flour with your fingertips until it resembles fine breadcrumbs. Stir in the cheese and mixed fresh herbs. Make a well in the centre, add the milk and mix with a flat-bladed knife until just combined. Bring the dough together into a rough ball, divide into eight portions and roll into small balls.

4 Add the dumplings to the soup, cover and simmer for 20 minutes, or until a skewer comes out clean when inserted into the centre of the dumplings. Season to taste and serve.

Note: The soup will keep in the refrigerator, covered, for up to 4 days, or in an airtight container in the freezer for up to 1 month.

SPICY CORN AND COCONUT SOUP

SERVES 4

1 tablespoon oil

1 large onion, chopped

1 celery stalk, chopped

2 garlic cloves, chopped

1 teaspoon ground coriander

1½ teaspoons ground cumin

1–2 teaspoons sambal oelek (see Note)

500 g (1 lb 2 oz) potatoes, chopped

750 ml (26 fl oz/3 cups) vegetable stock

420 g (14¾ oz) tin corn kernels, drained

270 ml (9½ fl oz) light coconut milk

1 handful coriander (cilantro) leaves

310 g (11 oz) tin creamed corn

extra coriander leaves, to serve

1 **Heat the oil** in a large heavy-based saucepan over medium–low heat. Add the onion, celery and garlic. Stir for 2 minutes to coat the vegetables in the oil. Reduce the heat, cover and simmer, stirring occasionally, for 5 minutes. Do not allow the vegetables to brown.

2 **Add the ground coriander,** cumin and 1 teaspoon of the sambal oelek and stir for 1 minute. Add the potato and stock. Bring slowly to the boil, then reduce the heat and simmer, covered, for 15 minutes, or until the potato is cooked.

3 **Stir in the corn kernels,** coconut milk and coriander leaves. Set aside to cool slightly.

4 **Using an immersion blender** fitted with the chopping blade, whizz the soup for 20–30 seconds, or until smooth. Stir in the creamed corn and gently reheat the soup. Add a little hot water if you prefer a thinner consistency. Season well with salt and freshly ground black pepper.

5 **Ladle into** four warm bowls and add the remaining sambal oelek, to taste. Sprinkle with the extra coriander leaves.

Note: Sambal oelek is a fiery condiment used in Malaysian, Indonesian and Singaporean cuisines. It is made from red chillies, vinegar and sugar and is available in jars from Asian supermarkets. The soup will keep in the refrigerator, covered, for up to 4 days, or in an airtight container in the freezer for up to 1 month.

SWEET POTATO, CHILLI AND CORIANDER SOUP

SERVES 4

6 whole coriander (cilantro) plants
(roots, stems and leaves)

1 small red chilli, seeded and
roughly chopped

2 garlic cloves, chopped

1 tablespoon oil

1 large onion, chopped

1 celery stalk, chopped

650 g (1 lb 7 oz) orange sweet potato,
cut into 5 cm (2 inch) pieces

1 litre (35 fl oz/4 cups) chicken stock or
vegetable stock

145 ml (4¾ fl oz) coconut milk

slices of toasted crusty bread, to serve

1   Remove the leaves from the coriander plants. Reserve a few whole leaves for garnishing and chop the remainder of the leaves. Set aside. Thoroughly wash the roots and stems and chop roughly. Put in a mini processor and add the chilli and garlic. Add 2 teaspoons of the oil and whizz for 20 seconds, or until the mixture forms a rough paste.

2   Heat the remaining oil in a large heavy-based saucepan. Add the paste and stir over low heat for 2 minutes, or until aromatic. Stir in the onion and celery. Cover and cook for 5 minutes, stirring once. Do not allow the mixture to brown.

3   Add the sweet potato and stir to coat in the mixture. Cook for 2 minutes, then add the stock. Bring to the boil, then reduce the heat, cover and cook for 20 minutes, or until the sweet potato is tender. Set aside to cool slightly.

4   Using an immersion blender fitted with the chopping blade, whizz the soup until smooth. Season well with salt and freshly ground black pepper. Stir in the coconut milk and gently reheat the soup. Add the chopped coriander leaves and serve garnished with the reserved whole coriander leaves.

5   Serve with slices of toasted crusty bread.

Note: The soup can also be served chilled. It will keep in the refrigerator, covered, for up to 5 days, or in an airtight container in the freezer for up to 1 month.

CHUNKY VEGETABLE SOUP

SERVES 6

100 g (3½ oz/½ cup) dried red kidney beans or borlotti beans

1 tablespoon olive oil

1 leek, halved lengthways, chopped

1 small onion, diced

2 carrots, chopped

2 celery sticks, chopped

1 large zucchini (courgette), chopped

1 tablespoon tomato paste (purée)

1 litre (35 fl oz/4 cups) vegetable stock

400 g (13 oz) pumpkin, cut into 2 cm (¾ inch) cubes

2 potatoes, cut into 2 cm (¾ inch) cubes

2 tablespoons chopped fresh flat-leaf (Italian) parsley

crusty wholemeal or wholegrain bread, to serve

1 Put the beans in a large bowl, cover with cold water and soak overnight. Rinse, then transfer to a saucepan, cover with cold water and cook for 45 minutes, or until just tender. Drain.

2 Heat the oil in a large saucepan. Add the leek and onion, and cook over medium heat for 2–3 minutes without browning, or until they start to soften.

3 Add the carrot, celery and zucchini, and cook for about 4 minutes. Add the tomato paste and stir for 1 minute.

4 Pour in the stock and 1.25 litres water, and bring to the boil. Reduce the heat to low and simmer for 20 minutes.

5 Add the pumpkin, potato, parsley and red kidney beans, and simmer for a further 20 minutes, or until the vegetables are tender and the beans are cooked. Season to taste.

6 Serve hot with crusty wholemeal or wholegrain bread.

Note: The soup will keep in the refrigerator, covered, for up to 4 days, or in an airtight container in the freezer for up to 1 month.

LENTIL AND VEGETABLE SOUP WITH SPICED YOGHURT

SERVES 6

2 tablespoons olive oil

1 small leek (white part only), chopped

2 garlic cloves, crushed

2 teaspoons curry powder

1 teaspoon ground cumin

1 teaspoon garam masala

1 litre (35 fl oz/4 cups) vegetable stock

1 fresh bay leaf

185 g (6 oz/1 cup) brown lentils

450 g (1 lb) butternut pumpkin (squash), peeled and cut into 1 cm (½ inch) cubes

400 g (14 oz) can chopped tomatoes

2 zucchini (courgettes), cut in half lengthways and sliced

200 g (7 oz) broccoli, cut into small florets

1 small carrot, diced

80 g (3 oz/½ cup) peas

1 tablespoon chopped mint

SPICED YOGHURT

250 g (1 cup) thick natural yoghurt

1 tablespoon chopped coriander (cilantro) leaves

1 garlic clove, crushed

3 dashes Tabasco sauce

1   Heat the oil in a saucepan over medium heat. Add the leek and garlic and cook for 4–5 minutes, or until soft and lightly golden.

2   Add the curry powder, cumin and garam masala and cook for 1 minute, or until the spices are fragrant.

3   Add the stock, bay leaf, lentils and pumpkin. Bring to the boil, then reduce the heat to low and simmer for 10–15 minutes, or until the lentils are tender. Season well.

4   Add the tomatoes, zucchini, broccoli, carrot and 500 ml (2 cups) water and simmer for 10 minutes, or until the vegetables are tender. Add the peas and simmer for 2–3 minutes.

5   To make the spiced yoghurt, place the yoghurt, coriander, garlic and Tabasco sauce in a small bowl and stir until combined.

6   Dollop a spoonful of the yoghurt on each serving of soup and garnish with the chopped mint.

Note: The soup will keep in the refrigerator, covered, for up to 5 days, or in an airtight container in the freezer for up to 1 month.

CARROT SOUP WITH CARAWAY BUTTER

CARAWAY BUTTER

1 tablespoon caraway seeds
125 g (4½ oz) butter, softened

1 onion, chopped
1 garlic clove, crushed
750 g (1 lb 10 oz) carrots, chopped
1 litre (35 fl oz/4 cups) vegetable stock
250 ml (9 fl oz/1 cup) orange juice
rye bread, to serve

1 To make the butter, dry-fry (see Note) the caraway seeds in a frying pan over medium heat for 3–4 minutes, or until they start to brown and release their aroma. Leave to cool and then grind in a spice grinder or coffee grinder until fine. Beat the butter and caraway together until smooth. Place in a small square of foil, roll into a log and refrigerate for 30 minutes, or until firm.

2 Put the onion, garlic, carrots, stock and orange juice into a saucepan and bring to the boil. Cover and simmer over a low heat for 25 minutes, or until the carrots are cooked.

3 Allow mixture to cool, then transfer to a blender and blend until smooth. Return to the pan, season to taste and heat through. Cut the butter into 5 mm (¼ inch) thick slices.

4 Spoon the soup into bowls, top each with two slices of the butter and serve with some rye bread.

Notes: Dry-frying is used to extract and bring out the flavour of whole spices, seeds or nuts. Fry them without fat in a heavy-bottomed pan over a high heat, shaking the pan from time to time. Continue cooking, watching carefully to avoid burning, until they give off a distinct aroma, and then tip them onto a cold plate. The soup will keep in the refrigerator, covered, for up to 4 days, or in an airtight container in the freezer for up to 1 month.

ROASTED TOMATO, ALMOND AND BASIL SOUP

SERVES 4

60 ml (2 fl oz/¼ cup) olive oil

1 kg (2 lb 4 oz) large, vine-ripened
tomatoes

1 large onion, finely chopped

2 garlic cloves, thinly sliced

50 g (1¾ oz/⅓ cup) blanched almonds,
roughly chopped

2 handfuls basil, roughly torn

750 ml (26 fl oz/3 cups) vegetable stock

slices of toasted crusty bread, to serve

1   Preheat the oven to 180°C (350°F/Gas 4). Grease a baking tray with 1 tablespoon of the oil. Cut the tomatoes in half, scoop out the seeds and arrange, cut side down, on the prepared tray. Roast for 15 minutes, then remove from the oven and set aside until the tomatoes are cool enough to handle. Discard the tomato skin and roughly chop the flesh.

2   Heat the remaining oil in a large saucepan over medium–low heat. Gently sauté the onion and garlic for 5–6 minutes, or until soft and translucent.

3   Add the chopped tomato, almonds and half the basil. Fry, stirring once or twice, for 5 minutes.

4   Transfer the mixture to a small processor fitted with the metal blade and whizz for 15–20 seconds, or until thick and smooth.

5   Return the mixture to the saucepan, stir in the stock and bring to the boil over medium–high heat.

6   Stir in the remaining basil, season with salt and freshly ground black pepper, to taste.

7   Serve immediately, with your choice of toasted crusty bread.

Note: The soup will keep in the refrigerator, covered, for up to 4 days, or in an airtight container in the freezer for up to 1 month.

LENTIL SOUP

SERVES 4

2 tablespoons olive oil

1 onion, finely chopped

1 leek, finely chopped

4 garlic cloves, finely chopped

1 tablespoon garam masala

1 stalk celery, finely diced

1 carrot, finely diced

230 g (8 oz/1¼ cups) brown lentils

400 g (14 oz) tin chopped tomatoes

1 tablespoon tomato paste
(concentrated purée)

1.75 litres (61 fl oz/7 cups) vegetable
stock

2 large sprigs thyme

2 tablespoons chopped parsley, to serve

grated parmesan cheese, to serve

1 Heat the oil in a large heavy-based saucepan. Add the onion, leek and garlic. Cook and stir for 2 minutes.

2 Add the garam masala and cook for a further 2 minutes.

3 Stir in the celery and carrot. Cover and cook, stirring two or three times, over low heat for 10 minutes, or until the vegetables are softened.

4 Add the lentils and stir to coat in the vegetables.

5 Add the tomatoes, tomato paste, stock and thyme sprigs. Bring to the boil, then lower the heat and simmer for 50 minutes, stirring occasionally, or until the lentils are tender. If evaporating too rapidly, add a little more stock or water to keep the lentils covered with liquid. Remove the thyme sprigs. Season well with salt and freshly ground black pepper.

6 Serve hot, sprinkled with parsley and parmesan.

Note: This is a very thick soup. You can thin it with a little stock or water, if desired. The soup will keep in the refrigerator, covered, for up to 4 days, or in an airtight container in the freezer for up to 1 month.

RED LENTIL, BURGHUL AND MINT SOUP

SERVES 4–6

2 tablespoons olive oil

1 large red onion, finely chopped

2 garlic cloves, crushed

2 tablespoons tomato paste (purée)

2 tomatoes, finely chopped

2 teaspoons paprika

1 teaspoon cayenne pepper

500 g (17 oz/2 cups) red lentils

50 g (2 oz/¼ cup) long-grain rice

2.25 litres (75 ml/8½ cups) vegetable stock

45 g (1½ oz/¼ cup) fine burghul (bulgar wheat)

2 tablespoons chopped mint

2 tablespoons chopped flat-leaf (Italian) parsley

90 g (3 oz/⅓ cup) thick natural yoghurt

¼ preserved lemon, pulp removed, zest washed and finely sliced

1 Heat the oil in a saucepan over medium heat. Add the onion and garlic and cook for 2–3 minutes, or until soft.

2 Stir in the tomato paste, tomato and spices and cook for 1 minute.

3 Add the lentils, rice and vegetable stock, then cover and bring to the boil over high heat. Reduce the heat and simmer for 30–35 minutes, or until the rice is cooked.

4 Stir in the burghul and herbs, then season to taste.

5 Divide the soup among serving bowls, garnish with yoghurt and preserved lemon.

6 Serve immediately.

Note: This soup will thicken on standing, so if reheating you may need to add more liquid. The soup will keep in the refrigerator, covered, for up to 4 days, or in an airtight container in the freezer for up to 1 month.

JERUSALEM ARTICHOKE SOUP

SERVES 4

50 g (1¾ oz) butter

1 onion, roughly chopped

1 leek, white part only, chopped

1 celery stalk, chopped

2 garlic cloves, chopped

800 g (1 lb 12 oz) Jerusalem artichokes, cut into 5 cm (2 inch) pieces

2 potatoes, about 250 g (9 oz), cut into 5 cm (2 inch) pieces

1 teaspoon freshly grated nutmeg

500 ml (17 fl oz/2 cups) vegetable stock

500 ml (17 fl oz/2 cups) milk

2 tablespoons finely snipped chives

slices of toasted crusty bread, to serve

1 **Heat the butter** in a large heavy-based saucepan over low heat. Add the onion, leek, celery and garlic and cook for 2 minutes. Cover and simmer, stirring occasionally, for 5 minutes. Do not allow the vegetables to brown.

2 **Add the Jerusalem artichokes**, potato and nutmeg and stir to combine. Cook for 2 minutes, then add the stock and 250 ml (9 fl oz/1 cup) of the milk. Bring to the boil, cover and cook for 20 minutes, or until the vegetables are tender.

3 **Remove the saucepan** from the heat. Using an immersion blender fitted with the chopping blade, whizz the soup for 10 seconds, or until roughly puréed. Season well with salt and freshly ground black pepper.

4 **Stir in the remaining milk** and half the chives and gently reheat the soup.

5 **Ladle the soup** into four bowls and sprinkle with the remaining chives and some freshly ground black pepper.

6 **Serve** immediately, with your choice of toasted crusty bread.

Notes: The Jerusalem artichokes can be replaced with an equal weight of potatoes. The soup will keep in the refrigerator, covered, for up to 4 days, or in an airtight container in the freezer for up to 1 month.

UDON NOODLE AND MUSHROOM SOUP

SERVES 4

1.5 litres (52 fl oz/6 cups) vegetable stock

2 tablespoons mirin

2 teaspoons grated fresh ginger

1 teaspoon wakame (dried seaweed) flakes

150 g (5½ oz) fresh shiitake mushrooms, sliced

440 g (15½ oz) packet fresh udon noodles

2 spring onions (scallions), sliced diagonally

75 g (2½ oz/¾ cup) snow peas (mangetout), trimmed and finely sliced lengthways

50 g (1¾ oz/½ cup) bean sprouts, trimmed

2 tablespoons light soy sauce

1 nori sheet, shredded

1 tablespoon shichimi togarashi (seven-spice blend – see Note), for sprinkling

1 **Put the stock** in a large saucepan and bring to the boil. Reduce the heat to a simmer.

2 **Add the mirin,** ginger, wakame and sliced mushrooms. Simmer for 5 minutes.

3 **Put the noodles** in a large bowl and pour over boiling water. Leave for 1 minute to heat through. Drain, refresh under cold running water and separate the noodles, then set aside.

4 **Add the spring onions,** snow peas, bean sprouts, soy sauce and shredded nori to the stock and simmer for a further 2 minutes.

5 **Divide the noodles** among four large serving bowls. Ladle over the hot broth and vegetables. Sprinkle with the shichimi togarashi to serve.

Note: Wakame flakes and nori are available from some supermarkets and Asian food stores. Shichimi togarashi is a Japanese seven-spice blend used to flavour noodles and soups. Typically, it contains red chilli pepper, orange peel, sesame seeds, seaweed, ginger and Japanese pepper. It is available from Japanese and Asian supermarkets. The soup should be eaten within 1 day. It is not suitable for freezing.

CHILLED CUCUMBER YOGHURT SOUP

SERVES 4

2 telegraph (long) cucumbers, about 550 g (1 lb 4 oz)

1 large handful mint

2 garlic cloves, chopped

1 teaspoon dried mint

125 ml (4 fl oz/½ cup) milk

500 g (1 lb 2 oz/2 cups) Greek-style yoghurt

2–3 teaspoons lemon juice, to taste

3–4 drops Tabasco sauce, to taste

2 tablespoons finely snipped chives, to serve

1 Peel the cucumbers, halve them lengthways and scoop out the seeds. Set aside about one-third of one of the cucumbers.

2 Put the remaining cucumber in a small processor fitted with the metal blade. Add the mint, garlic, dried mint and milk and whizz in 3–4 second bursts for 20 seconds.

3 Add the yoghurt, and the lemon juice and Tabasco sauce to taste, and season well with salt and freshly ground black pepper. Whizz until well combined and smooth.

4 Transfer the soup to a bowl, cover and refrigerate for at least 2 hours to allow the flavours to develop.

5 Finely dice the reserved cucumber.

6 Ladle the soup into bowls and top with the diced cucumber and chives.

Note: The soup should be eaten within 1 day. It is not suitable for freezing.

SIDES

ROASTED POTATO CAKE

SERVES 6–8

oil, for brushing

250 g (9 oz/1 cup) light sour cream

3 tablespoons milk

1 kg (2 lb 4 oz) all-purpose potatoes

150 g (5½ oz/1¼ cups) grated cheddar cheese

50 g (1¾ oz/½ cup) grated parmesan cheese

6 spring onions (scallions), finely chopped

pinch of cayenne pepper

1 Preheat a kettle or covered barbecue to medium indirect heat. Brush a 26 cm (10½ inch) round shallow cake tin with oil. Fold a 30 cm (12 inch) sheet of foil in half and use it to line the cake tin, running the edges up the sides of the tin. Brush the foil with oil, then line the base with a sheet of baking paper.

2 In a large bowl, stir the sour cream and milk together until smooth.

3 Peel the potatoes and slice them very thinly using a food processor or mandolin. Gently mix the potato through the sour cream mixture along with the cheddar, 4 tablespoons of the parmesan, the spring onion and cayenne pepper. Season well with salt and freshly ground black pepper.

4 Tip the mixture into the prepared tin, pressing down firmly with the back of a spoon. Scatter the remaining parmesan over the top and cover the tin with foil.

5 Put the tin on the barbecue, then lower the lid and cook the potato cake for 45 minutes. Remove the foil covering and continue baking for 45 minutes, or until the top of the potato is golden and crisp. Leave for 5 minutes, then gently loosen the potato cake out of the tin, using the foil wings as handles.

6 Cut into serving portions and serve hot.

Note: This dish can also be cooked in a preheated 200°C (400°F) oven for about 45 minutes, or until crisp and golden.

GRILLED MIXED VEGETABLES

SERVES 4

1 red capsicum (pepper)

1 yellow capsicum (pepper)

2 zucchini (courgettes), halved

4 button mushrooms, quartered

1 onion, cut into wedges

140 g (5 oz) jap (kent) pumpkin, cut into 4 thin slices

4 garlic cloves

2 tablespoons ready-made pesto

2 tablespoons extra virgin olive oil

35 g (1¼ oz/⅓ cup) shaved parmesan cheese

1 Heat the grill (broiler) to high.

2 Cut the capsicums into large flat pieces and remove the seeds and membranes. Cook, skin side up, under the hot grill until the skin blackens and blisters. Leave to cool in a plastic bag.

3 While the capsicum is cooling, spread the zucchini, mushroom, onion and pumpkin on the grill tray and grill for 12 minutes, or until cooked. Remove from the grill and allow to cool.

4 Peel the skin from the cooled capsicum and gently toss the flesh in a large serving bowl with all the other grilled vegetables.

5 In a small bowl, combine the pesto and oil. Season to taste with salt and freshly ground black pepper and drizzle over the vegetables. Gently toss together, scatter with the parmesan and serve.

ASPARAGUS WITH PARMESAN AND SUMAC

SERVES 4

350 g (12 oz/2 bunches) asparagus, trimmed

2 tablespoons virgin olive oil

40 g (1½ oz) butter

2 garlic cloves, crushed

1 teaspoon sumac, optional (see Note)

4 Roma (plum) tomatoes, peeled, seeded and chopped

2 tablespoons snipped chives

50 g (1¾ oz/½ cup) freshly grated parmesan cheese

1   **Heat the grill** (broiler) to very hot. Bring a saucepan of lightly salted water to the boil, add the asparagus spears and blanch for 1 minute. Drain well, refresh under cold water and pat dry with paper towels.

2   **Put the oil in a large,** shallow ovenproof dish, add the asparagus spears and roll them around in the oil. Place the dish under the grill and cook the asparagus for 3–4 minutes, or until tender, turning once.

3   **Meanwhile,** melt the butter in a saucepan. Add the garlic and sumac and cook over medium heat for 1 minute, or until fragrant. Remove from the heat, stir in the tomato and chives and season to taste.

4   **Spoon the mixture** over the asparagus, scatter with the parmesan and grill for another 3 minutes, or until the cheese has melted. Serve immediately.

Note: Sumac is a purple-red spice with a mild lemony flavour available from Middle Eastern grocery stores and gourmet food shops. If you can't obtain any, you could use ½ teaspoon sweet paprika in this recipe instead.

PUMPKIN WITH SAFFRON AND CORIANDER BUTTER

SERVES 6

SAFFRON AND CORIANDER BUTTER

small pinch of saffron threads

50 g (1¾ oz) butter, softened

1 tablespoon finely chopped coriander
(cilantro) leaves

½ jap (kent) pumpkin

olive oil, for brushing

3 tablespoons coriander (cilantro) leaves

1 To make saffron and coriander butter, put the saffron in a small bowl, add 2 teaspoons of hot water and leave to soak for at least 20 minutes. Add butter and coriander and mix until thoroughly combined. Put the butter mixture into the centre of a piece of plastic wrap. Roll it up into a 7 cm (2¾ inch) log. Refrigerate for about 30 minutes, or until firm.

2 Preheat a barbecue grill plate or chargrill pan to high. Slice the unpeeled pumpkin into 2 cm (¾ inch) thick wedges and discard the seeds. Brush the wedges on both sides with oil and season with salt and freshly ground black pepper.

3 Grill the pumpkin for 10 minutes on each side, or until browned and tender.

4 Place on a serving platter and top with the sliced saffron and coriander butter. Allow the butter to melt a little and serve the pumpkin hot, scattered with coriander leaves.

RED VEGETABLES WITH HERB BUTTER

SERVES 4

40 g (1½ oz) butter, softened

3 tablespoons basil leaves, chopped

1 red capsicum (pepper), quartered

2 small beetroot, quartered, or 4 baby
    beets, halved

4 garlic cloves, unpeeled

4 cherry tomato trusses, each with
    3 tomatoes attached

2 tablespoons oil

4 thyme sprigs

4 tablespoons vegetable stock

1 **In a small bowl,** combine the butter and basil and season with salt and freshly ground black pepper. Turn out onto a piece of foil and form into an 8 cm (3¼ inch) long log. Roll up tightly and freeze for 30 minutes.

2 **Meanwhile,** preheat a kettle or covered barbecue to low indirect heat.

3 **Put the capsicum,** beetroot, garlic cloves and the cherry tomato trusses in a large bowl. Drizzle with the oil, then lightly toss. Lay 4 large sheets of foil on a flat surface and divide the vegetable mixture evenly among the sheets. Add a sprig of thyme to each, then 1 tablespoon of stock and tightly fold up each parcel to secure.

4 **Put the parcels on the barbecue grill,** then lower the lid and cook for 30 minutes, or until the vegetables are tender. Cut the butter into 1 cm (½ inch) thick slices, then open up the parcels and divide the butter among them while they're still on the barbecue. Cook for a further 1–2 minutes to melt the butter, then serve.

SKEWERED GARLIC AND CUMIN MUSHROOMS

SERVES 4

16 button mushrooms

4 tablespoons olive oil

1 garlic clove, crushed

½ teaspoon ground cumin

2 tablespoons chopped parsley

1 lemon, cut into 4 wedges

1 Soak four bamboo skewers in cold water for 30 minutes. Preheat a barbecue grill plate, flat plate or chargrill pan to medium.

2 Trim the ends of the mushroom stalks, but don't cut them off completely. Put the oil, garlic, cumin and some salt and freshly ground black pepper in a bowl. Add the mushrooms and toss to coat.

3 Thread 4 mushrooms onto each skewer, piercing them through the stalk.

4 Barbecue the mushrooms, turning occasionally and brushing with any remaining oil mixture, for about 5 minutes, or until soft and lightly browned.

5 Place on a serving plate, sprinkle with parsley, add a squeeze of lemon and serve.

ASIAN VEGETABLES

SERVES 4

30 g (1 oz) lily buds (see Notes)

20 g (¾ oz) fresh black fungus
(wood ears)

8 large dried shiitake mushrooms

2 tablespoons vegetable or peanut oil

2 garlic cloves, chopped

½ red capsicum (pepper), sliced

200 g (7 oz) tin fried gluten, drained
(see Note)

2½ tablespoons oyster sauce

2 teaspoons soy sauce

1 teaspoon sugar

1 **Soak the lily buds** and black fungus separately in warm water for 15 minutes, then drain.

2 **Soak the dried** shiitake mushrooms in 125 ml (4 fl oz/½ cup) of hot water for 10 minutes. Drain. Discard the woody stems and chop the caps in half.

3 **Heat the oil** in a wok over medium heat. Add the garlic and capsicum and stir-fry for 1 minute. Add the lily buds, black fungus, mushrooms and gluten. Toss well for another minute. Stir in the oyster sauce, soy sauce and sugar and mix gently until combined.

4 **Delicious served** with steamed rice.

Notes: Lily buds (also known as golden needles) are the unopened flowers of day lilies. The buds are usually bought dried and then soaked, but are sometimes available fresh from Chinese markets. They have an earthy flavour and are used mainly in Chinese vegetarian dishes, or in stir-fries. Fried gluten is sold in tins or bottles in Asian shops, and is usually used as a substitute for meat, due to its 'meaty' texture.

PUMPKINS WITH GOAT'S CHEESE AND MACADAMIAS

SERVES 4

2 x 350 g (12 oz) golden nugget pumpkins (miniki squash)

1 tablespoon oil

40 g (1½ oz/1 cup) baby rocket (arugula) leaves

35 g (1¼ oz/¼ cup) chopped roasted macadamia nuts

80 g (2¾ oz) goat's cheese, crumbled

HONEY MUSTARD DRESSING

3 tablespoons olive oil

1 tablespoon sherry vinegar

2 teaspoons wholegrain mustard

1 teaspoon honey

1 Preheat a kettle or covered barbecue to medium indirect heat.

2 Wash the pumpkins thoroughly, then cut them in half horizontally and remove all the seeds. Rub the oil all over the flesh and place the pumpkins cut side up in a disposable foil tray. Season lightly with salt and freshly ground black pepper.

3 Put the tray on the barbecue grill, then lower the lid and cook for 30 minutes, or until browned and soft — the cooking time will depend on the thickness of your pumpkins.

4 Meanwhile, put all the honey mustard dressing ingredients in a small screw-top jar. Shake well to combine and season to taste with salt and freshly ground black pepper.

5 Put the rocket, macadamia nuts and goat's cheese in a large bowl and gently mix together. Add the dressing and toss lightly to combine.

6 Fill the cooked pumpkin halves with the salad mixture and serve immediately.

Note: The skin of the pumpkins can be eaten in this recipe — just be sure to wash the pumpkins well before cooking.

GRILLED GREEN TOMATOES WITH WALNUT CRUMBLE

SERVES 4–6

4 green tomatoes (see Note)

75 g (2½ oz/1 cup) coarse fresh breadcrumbs, made from an Italian bread such as ciabatta

1 garlic clove, crushed

2 tablespoons roughly chopped walnuts

40 g (1½ oz) butter, melted

2 tablespoons roughly chopped flat-leaf (Italian) parsley

1 tablespoon roughly chopped oregano

2 tablespoons grated parmesan cheese

1   Heat the grill (broiler) to medium. Cut each tomato into six wedges, remove the core and sit the wedges in a shallow, lightly oiled 17 x 26 cm (6½ x 10½ inch) ovenproof dish. Put the dish under the grill and cook the tomato for 5 minutes, or until heated through, turning the wedges over once during cooking.

2   **Combine all the remaining ingredients** in a bowl and add salt and freshly ground black pepper to taste.

3   **Sprinkle the mixture** over the tomatoes and grill for another 5–6 minutes, or until the topping is golden brown and the tomatoes are hot. Serve hot.

Note: The green tomatoes used in this recipe are simply unripe regular tomatoes. They can be difficult to find, so you may need to ask your greengrocer to order some in for you.

CAULIFLOWER AND PEAS WITH A POLONAISE TOPPING

SERVES 4

1 small cauliflower, cut into small florets

150 g (5½ oz/1 cup) fresh or frozen peas (see Note)

POLONAISE TOPPING

3 hard-boiled eggs

40 g (1½ oz/½ cup) fresh white breadcrumbs

1½ tablespoons baby capers, rinsed and drained

3 tablespoons finely chopped flat-leaf (Italian) parsley

1 garlic clove, finely chopped

75 g (2½ oz) unsalted butter, melted

1 Heat the grill (broiler) to high.

2 Add the cauliflower and peas to a large saucepan of lightly salted boiling water and simmer for about 5 minutes, or until tender. Drain the vegetables and arrange in a lightly oiled 26 x 18 cm (10½ × 7 inch) gratin dish.

3 While the vegetables are cooking, make the polonaise topping. Mash the eggs in a bowl using a fork, then add the breadcrumbs, capers, parsley, garlic and melted butter. Mix well and season to taste with salt and freshly ground black pepper.

4 Sprinkle the topping all over the vegetables and grill for about 5–7 minutes, or until the breadcrumbs are golden and crunchy. Serve hot.

Note: If you prefer to use fresh peas in this recipe, you will need to pod about 300 g (10½ oz/2 cups) fresh peas to get the right amount.

SPICED POTATOES

SERVES 6

1.5 kg (3 lb 5 oz) roasting potatoes, peeled, cut into 4 cm (1½ inch) pieces

2 tablespoons ghee (clarified butter – see Note)

2 teaspoons ground fenugreek

1 garlic clove, crushed

1 teaspoon finely grated fresh ginger

1 tablespoon black mustard seeds

pinch saffron threads

80 g (2¾ oz) baby English spinach leaves

1 **Preheat the oven** to 180°C (350°F/Gas 4). Boil, steam or microwave the potatoes until just tender, then drain well.

2 **Melt the ghee** in a small frying pan over medium heat. Cook the fenugreek, garlic, ginger, mustard seeds and saffron. Season with salt and stir, for about 1 minute, or until fragrant.

3 **Place potatoes** in a large roasting pan, add the spice mixture and toss to coat the potatoes. Bake for about 1 hour, or until the potatoes are lightly browned. Remove from the oven, toss the spinach through the potatoes. Serve immediately.

Note: Ghee is clarified butter, the butter oil, without the lactose and other milk solids. It is traditionally prepared by gently heating butter until it becomes a clear golden liquid. The lactose and other milk solids coagulate and are meticulously removed. This process also evaporates most of the natural water content, making ghee light, pure and resistant to spoilage.

QUICK VEGETABLE STIR-FRY

SERVES 4

2 tablespoons oil

2 garlic cloves, finely chopped

2 teaspoons finely chopped fresh ginger

1 carrot, sliced

1 red capsicum (pepper), sliced

200 g (7 oz) broccoli, cut into florets

115 g (4 oz/ 2/3 cup) fresh baby corn, cut in half diagonally

300 g (10½ oz) Chinese cabbage (wong bok), cut into 2.5 cm (1 inch) pieces

100 g (3½ oz/1 cup) snowpeas (mangetout), topped and tailed

2 tablespoons oyster sauce

2 teaspoons soy sauce

1 teaspoon sugar

¼ teaspoon sesame oil

2 teaspoons cornflour (cornstarch) mixed with 1 tablespoon water, to thicken (optional)

1 Heat the oil in a wok over high heat, add the garlic and ginger and cook until aromatic. Add the carrot and capsicum and stir-fry for 1 minute, then add the broccoli and toss for 1–2 minutes. Add the baby corn and cabbage and stir-fry until the cabbage starts to wilt and soften (this will take about 1½ minutes).

2 Toss in the snowpeas and cook for another minute. By this time the vegetables should have a glossy sheen and be partially cooked, with a slight crunch in them.

3 Reduce the heat and add the oyster sauce, soy sauce, sugar and the sesame oil. Toss well to coat. Add the cornflour mixture to thicken slightly if you wish.

4 Serve hot as a side dish or with steamed rice or noodles.

TOMATO, EGGPLANT AND OLIVE CAPONATA

SERVES 4

3 firm tomatoes

5 bulb spring onions (scallions), trimmed but not peeled

3 slender eggplants (aubergines), cut lengthways into 5 mm (¼ inch) thick slices

2 red capsicums (peppers), quartered

50 g (1¾ oz/⅓ cup) pitted kalamata olives

1 tablespoon toasted pine nuts

3 tablespoons torn mint leaves

3 tablespoons olive oil

3 teaspoons white wine vinegar

1 teaspoon caster (superfine) sugar

1 garlic clove, crushed

1 **Heat the grill** (broiler) to high and line the grill tray with foil. Sit the whole tomatoes and onions on the rack of the grill tray and cook for about 10 minutes, turning often, until the tomato skins are charred in patches all over and start to split.

2 **Remove the tomatoes** from the heat and put the eggplant and capsicum on the rack, skin side up. Grill for about 8 minutes, or until well browned, turning the eggplant halfway through cooking. Remove all the vegetables from the grill and put the capsicum in a plastic bag to sweat.

3 **Peel the tomatoes,** cut them into 2 cm (¾ inch) chunks and place in a colander to drain.

4 **Cut the eggplant** into thick strips and put them in a bowl.

5 **When the capsicum** is cool enough to handle, peel off the skin, then cut the flesh into strips.

6 **Halve the onions** from top to bottom, then give them a light squeeze so that the centre pops out.

7 **Add the capsicum** and onion to the eggplant along with the olives, pine nuts and mint and gently stir together.

8 **Put the oil,** vinegar, sugar and garlic in a small screw-top jar and shake well to combine. Season liberally with salt and freshly ground black pepper and drizzle over the grilled vegetables. Add the drained tomato. Toss lightly and serve at room temperature.

GRILLED CAPSICUM, PECAN AND HERB SALSA

SERVES 4

2 red capsicums (peppers)

2 yellow capsicums (peppers)

1 small red chilli, seeded and finely chopped

50 g (1¾ oz/½ cup) pecan nuts, halved lengthways

2 spring onions (scallions), finely chopped

juice of 1 lime

2 tablespoons olive oil

1 handful mint leaves

2 handfuls coriander (cilantro) leaves

thick plain yoghurt, optional, to serve

1 Heat the grill (broiler) to high. Cut the capsicums into large flat pieces and remove the seeds and membranes. Cook, skin-side-up, under the hot grill until the skin blackens and blisters. Leave to cool in a plastic bag, then peel away the skin and cut the capsicum into 2 cm (¾ inch) squares.

2 Gently toss the capsicum in a serving bowl with all the remaining ingredients.

3 Serve the salsa at room temperature, with a dollop of yoghurt if desired, seasoned with salt and freshly ground black pepper.

STIR-FRIED CAULIFLOWER WITH CASHEW NUTS

SERVES 4

1 tablespoon vegetable or peanut oil

1 onion, cut into thin wedges

2 garlic cloves, crushed

1 tablespoon Madras curry powder or
mild curry powder

2 teaspoons mild curry paste

500 g (1 lb 2 oz/4 cups) cauliflower, cut
into small florets

2 tomatoes, cut into wedges

125 ml (4 fl oz/½ cup) chicken or
vegetable stock

2 teaspoons tomato paste (concentrate
purée)

3 tablespoons thick coconut cream

100 g (3½ oz/⅔ cup) unsalted toasted
cashew nuts, roughly chopped

coriander (cilantro) leaves, to garnish

1 **Heat a wok** over high heat, add the oil and swirl to coat. Add the onion and stir-fry for 1–2 minutes, or until golden. Add the garlic, curry powder and curry paste and stir-fry for 1 minute. Stir in the cauliflower and toss until well coated.

2 **Add the tomato, stock,** tomato paste and coconut cream and stir-fry for about 5–6 minutes, or until well combined and the cauliflower is cooked. Toss through the nuts just before serving and serve garnished with the coriander leaves.

WATER SPINACH IN FLAMES

SERVES 4

2 tablespoons yellow bean sauce (taucheo)

1 tablespoon fish sauce or light soy sauce

2 tablespoons oil

500 g (1 lb 2 oz) water spinach (ong choy), cut into 3 cm (1¼ inch) lengths

3 garlic cloves, crushed

4 red Asian shallots, finely sliced

1 **Combine the yellow bean sauce** and fish sauce (or light soy sauce) in a small bowl.

2 **Heat a wok** over high heat, add the oil and swirl to coat. Stir-fry the water spinach for 1 minute, or until slightly wilted.

3 **Add the garlic** and shallots and cook for 15 seconds, then stir in the sauce and toss for 30 seconds, or until the leaves are well coated and the stems are tender. Serve immediately.

EGGPLANT STACKS

SERVES 4

1 small eggplant (aubergine), cut into 4 thick slices

oil, for brushing

2 vine-ripened tomatoes, quartered

150 g (5½ oz) rocket (arugula) leaves

150 g (5½ oz) bocconcini (fresh baby mozzarella) cheese, sliced

4 tablespoons virgin olive oil

1 tablespoon white wine vinegar

1 garlic clove, crushed

6 kalamata olives, pitted and finely chopped

2 tablespoons finely chopped basil leaves

1 Heat the grill (broiler) to high. Brush the eggplant slices generously with oil. Place on the grill tray, season with salt and freshly ground black pepper and grill for about 10 minutes, or until lightly browned and almost cooked through, turning once during cooking.

2 Add the tomato to the grill tray, lightly brush with oil and season with salt and freshly ground black pepper. Grill for another 2 minutes, then remove the tomato and eggplant from the heat and leave to cool.

3 To assemble the stacks, arrange the rocket leaves on four serving plates. Add an eggplant slice, and top each with some tomato and bocconcini.

4 In a small bowl, whisk together the oil, vinegar and garlic. Add the olives and season to taste. Spoon over the stacks, sprinkle with the basil and serve warm.

ROOT VEGETABLES WITH CARAWAY AND GARLIC OIL

SERVES 4

2 bulbs beetroot, cut into thick wedges

2 parsnips, cut in half lengthways

1 swede (rutabaga), cut into thick wedges

4 carrots, cut in half lengthways

1½ tablespoons caraway seeds

10 garlic cloves, unpeeled

3 tablespoons olive oil

2 slices day-old caraway bread, crusts removed

2 tablespoons roughly snipped garlic chives

1   Parboil the beetroot for 20 minutes, or until tender, then drain. Preheat the oven to 200°C (400°F/Gas 6).

2   In a large roasting pan, toss all the vegetables with the caraway seeds, garlic and 2 tablespoons olive oil. Season with salt and freshly ground black pepper. Roast for 30 minutes, then turn the vegetables. Reduce heat to 180°C (350°F/Gas 4) and roast for a further 30–40 minutes, or until golden.

3   Meanwhile, brush the bread on both sides lightly with the remaining oil. Place on a baking tray and bake for 30 minutes, turning after 15 minutes, until crisp and golden. Cool, then break into chunky breadcrumbs.

4   Remove from the oven and serve on a platter sprinkled with the caraway breadcrumbs and garlic chives.

Note: If you can't get caraway bread, use plain bread, and increase the caraway seeds to 2 tablespoons.

GRILLED MIXED MUSHROOMS

SERVES 4

2 field mushrooms

150 g (6 oz) fresh
  shiitake mushrooms

100 g (3 oz) enoki mushrooms

150 g (6 oz) oyster mushrooms

150 g (6 oz) shimeji mushrooms

50 g (1¾ oz) butter, melted

2 tablespoons Japanese soy sauce

1 tablespoon mirin

1 tablespoon chopped flat-leaf (Italian)
  parsley

1   Heat the grill (broiler) to medium.

2   While the grill is heating, prepare the mushrooms. Discard the stems from the field mushrooms and cut the caps into quarters. Discard the stems from the shiitake mushrooms and cut the shiitake in half. Trim the hard ends off the enoki and pull apart the mushroom tops. Gently tear apart the oyster mushrooms. Remove the rough ends from the shimeji stems and gently pull apart the caps. Put all the mushrooms in a large bowl.

3   Combine the butter, soy sauce and mirin in a small bowl, pour over the mushrooms and toss to combine.

4   Place the mushrooms in a shallow ovenproof dish, put the dish under the grill and cook the mushrooms for 5 minutes.

5   Remove from the heat and gently toss the mushrooms with a pair of tongs, then grill for another 5 minutes. Serve hot, scattered with the parsley.

ASIAN GREENS WITH CHILLI AND COCONUT MARINADE

SERVES 4

MARINADE

15 g (½ oz/¼ cup) shredded coconut

2 garlic cloves, roughly chopped

2 cm (¾ inch) piece ginger, roughly chopped

1 red Asian shallot, roughly chopped

1 small red chilli, sliced

2 tablespoons oil

1 tablespoon rice vinegar

2 teaspoons fish sauce or light soy sauce

1 teaspoon soft brown sugar

2 spring onions (scallions), sliced

1.1 kg (2 lb 7 oz) Asian green vegetables

vegetable oil, for cooking

sesame oil, to serve (optional)

1 **To make the marinade,** heat a dry frying pan over medium heat. Add the shredded coconut and fry, stirring, for 3–4 minutes, or until brown. Transfer the coconut to a spice mill or mini processor, add the garlic, ginger, shallot and chilli and whizz until finely chopped. Add the oil, vinegar, fish sauce (or light soy sauce) and sugar and whizz in short bursts until blended. Transfer to a large bowl and stir in the spring onion.

2 **Slice the Asian green vegetables** into 8 cm (3¼ inch) lengths and divide these into stems and leaves. Heat a wok or large frying pan over medium–high heat and add 2 tablespoons of vegetable oil. Add the vegetable stems and stir-fry for 1 minute. Add the vegetable leaves and stir-fry for 45–60 seconds, or until they wilt and turn bright green.

3 **Transfer the hot vegetables** to the bowl with the marinade and toss to coat. Marinate for at least 1 hour to allow the flavours to develop.

4 **Serve the vegetables** cold or reheat them in the wok. Drizzle with a little sesame oil, if using.

SPICED BASMATI AND NUT RICE

SERVES 4

small pinch saffron threads

250 g (9 oz/1¼ cups) basmati rice

2 tablespoons vegetable oil

2 cinnamon sticks

6 green cardamom pods, crushed

6 cloves

75 g (2½ oz/½ cup) blanched almonds, toasted

75 g (2½ oz/scant ⅔ cup) raisins

1 teaspoon salt

2 tablespoons chopped coriander (cilantro) leaves

1 **Soak the saffron threads** in 3 tablespoons of boiling water until required.

2 **Put the rice in a sieve** and wash under cold running water until the water runs clear.

3 **Heat the oil in a saucepan,** add the spices and fry gently over medium heat for 1–2 minutes, or until they start to release their aroma.

4 **Add the rice,** nuts and raisins and stir well until all the grains are glossy.

5 **Add 500 ml** (17 fl oz/2 cups) of cold water and the salt and bring to the boil. Cover and simmer gently over low heat for 15 minutes.

6 **Remove the pan** from the heat, remove the lid, and drizzle over the saffron water. Cover and leave to stand for a further 10 minutes. Stir through the coriander and serve.

ASPARAGUS WITH A CREAMY LEMON-PEPPER DRESSING

SERVES 4

4 tablespoons extra virgin olive oil

2 tablespoons lemon juice

3 tablespoons crème fraîche or sour cream, softened

20 asparagus spears

1 Preheat a barbecue grill plate or flat plate to medium.

2 In a small bowl, combine the oil and lemon juice, and season well with salt and freshly ground black pepper. Pour half the mixture into a shallow dish for coating the asparagus.

3 Stir the crème fraîche through the remaining mixture, then season to taste and set aside.

4 Snap off and discard the tough ends from the asparagus spears. Put the spears in the shallow dish with the oil and lemon juice mixture and roll them around to coat.

5 Cook the asparagus on the hotplate, turning frequently with tongs, for about 4–5 minutes, or until just tender and lightly charred. If any spears begin to brown too quickly, move them to the outside of the barbecue.

6 Put the asparagus on a serving platter, pour the reserved crème fraîche dressing over the spears and serve.

INDIAN CAULIFLOWER WITH MUSTARD SEEDS

SERVES 6

4 tablespoons vegetable oil

1 tablespoon cumin seeds

1 tablespoon mustard seeds

1 teaspoon chilli powder

1 teaspoon ground turmeric

½ teaspoon salt

1 kg (2 lb 4 oz) cauliflower, cut into small florets

90 g (3¼ oz/⅓ cup) Greek-style yoghurt

juice of ½ lemon

7 large handfuls coriander (cilantro) leaves

1 **Heat the oil** in a large wok over medium–high heat. Add the cumin seeds and mustard seeds. Cook, tossing, for 1 minute, or until the mustard seeds start to pop.

2 **Stir in the chilli powder**, turmeric and salt.

3 **Add the cauliflower florets** to the wok and toss to coat in the spice mix. Cover and reduce the heat to medium. Cook for 10 minutes, tossing about every 2 minutes, or until the cauliflower is tender. Remove from the heat.

4 **Add the yoghurt and lemon juice** to the wok. Toss to coat. Toss in the coriander ans serve immediately.

POLENTA WITH CORN, TOMATO AND AVOCADO SALSA

SERVES 4

225 g (8 oz/1½ cups) instant polenta

40 g (1½ oz) butter, chopped

2 garlic cloves, crushed

olive oil, for brushing

CORN, TOMATO AND AVOCADO SALSA

2 small corn cobs, husks and silks removed

2 tomatoes, diced

1 small avocado, diced

1 teaspoon lime juice

1 tablespoon olive oil

1   First, prepare the polenta. Bring 1 litre (35 fl oz/4 cups) of water to the boil in a saucepan. Add 2 teaspoons of salt and gradually add the polenta in a steady stream, stirring constantly. Reduce the heat to low and cook, stirring often, until all the liquid is absorbed and the mixture comes away from the sides of the pan. This will take about 3–4 minutes. Stir in the butter and garlic and immediately pour into a lightly oiled, shallow 22 cm (8½ inch) square cake tin. Level the surface with the back of a wet spoon, and leave to cool at room temperature for 20–30 minutes.

2   Preheat a barbecue grill plate to medium. Lightly brush with oil and cook the corn cobs, turning often, for about 8–10 minutes, or until tender and lightly browned. Take them off the heat and when they're cool enough to handle, slice the kernels off the cobs and put them in a bowl.

3   Add the remaining salsa ingredients, season with salt and plenty of freshly ground black pepper, then toss together lightly.

4   Turn the cooled polenta out onto a flat surface and cut it into four squares. Cut each in half to give eight rectangles. Brush both sides well with some olive oil and barbecue for 3 minutes, or until grill lines appear. Turn and cook the other side for another 3 minutes, or until grill lines appear.

5   Divide the polenta between four serving plates and top with a spoonful of salsa. Serve at once.

CHINESE BROCCOLI AND SESAME STIR-FRY

SERVES 4

1 tablespoon vegetable or peanut oil

3 garlic cloves, crushed

1.5 kg (3 lb 5 oz/2 bunches) Chinese broccoli (gai lan), cut into thirds

2 teaspoons sesame oil

3 tablespoons oyster sauce

2 tablespoons toasted sesame seeds

1 **Heat a wok** over high heat, add the oil and swirl to coat. Cook the garlic for about 30 seconds.

2 **Add the Chinese** broccoli and 2 tablespoons of water and stir-fry for 3–4 minutes, or until the broccoli has wilted and the water has evaporated.

3 **Add the sesame oil** and oyster sauce and stir-fry for 1 minute, or until coated.

4 **Serve** sprinkled with sesame seeds.

BIRYANI-STYLE RICE

SERVES 4

200 g (7 oz/1 cup) basmati rice

pinch of saffron threads

1 cinnamon stick

4 cardamom pods, smashed

1 large potato, cut into 2 cm (¾ inch) cubes

1 teaspoon sea salt

3 tablespoons vegetable or peanut oil

1 eggplant (aubergine), cut into 2 cm (¾ inch) cubes

1 red onion, cut into thin wedges

3 garlic cloves, crushed

1 tablespoon grated fresh ginger

1 teaspoon dried chilli flakes

1 teaspoon ground cinnamon

1 teaspoon ground coriander

2 teaspoons ground cumin

1 teaspoon ground cardamom

1 teaspoon fennel seeds, ground

155 g (5½ oz/1¼ cups) green beans, trimmed and cut into 2 cm (¾ inch) lengths, blanched

100 g (3½ oz/⅔ cup) frozen peas, thawed

50 g (1¾ oz/⅓ cup) currants

1 small handful coriander (cilantro) leaves

2 tablespoons chopped toasted pistachio kernels

1 **Wash the rice** under cold water until it runs clear.

2 **Put the rice,** saffron, cinnamon, cardamom pods, potato cubes and salt in a large saucepan. Fill with cold water to 2 cm (¾ inch) above the rice and bring to a simmer over low heat. When the rice starts to pocket (after about 5 minutes), cover and cook for 10 minutes, or until the rice is tender. Fluff the rice with a fork and turn out onto a flat tray to cool slightly. Discard the cinnamon stick and cardamom pods.

3 **Heat a wok** over high heat, add 2 tablespoons of the oil and swirl to coat. Add the eggplant and stir-fry for 3–4 minutes, or until softened and golden. Remove from the wok.

4 **Heat the remaining oil** in the wok, add the onion and cook for 1 minute, or until softened. Add the garlic, ginger, chilli, spices and beans and cook for 1 minute. Stir in the rice mixture, eggplant, peas, currants and coriander leaves and gently toss until combined. Serve sprinkled with pistachios.

GRILLED EGGPLANT WITH MISO AND PARMESAN

SERVES 4

6 slender eggplants (aubergines)

2 teaspoons light olive oil

1½ tablespoons white miso paste

1 tablespoon mirin

1 egg yolk

2 tablespoons finely grated parmesan cheese

2 tablespoons snipped chives

1 Heat the grill (broiler) to high. Slice the eggplants in half lengthways and prick the skins several times with a fork. Brush the eggplant with the oil, place skin-side-up on the grill tray and grill for 10 minutes, turning once.

2 Remove the eggplant from the grill and arrange in a shallow ovenproof serving dish. Turn the grill down to medium.

3 Put the miso paste, mirin and egg yolk in a small bowl and whisk well to combine. Pour the mixture evenly over the surface of the eggplant and put the dish under the grill. Cook for 2 minutes, then sprinkle with the parmesan and grill for 1 minute more, or until the cheese starts to turn golden. Sprinkle with the chives and serve.

TOMATOES STUFFED WITH PISTACHIO COUSCOUS

MAKES 8

200 g (7 oz) instant couscous

40 g (1½ oz) butter

100 g (3½ oz/⅔ cup) currants

1½ teaspoons grated orange zest

4 tablespoons orange juice

75 g (2½ oz/½ cup) pistachio nuts, roughly chopped

50 g (1¾ oz/½ cup) grated parmesan cheese

1 large handful basil leaves, chopped

8 firm vine-ripened tomatoes

1 **Preheat a kettle** or covered barbecue to low indirect heat.

2 **Put the couscous in a heatproof bowl** and pour on 500 ml (17 fl oz/2 cups) boiling water. Stir briefly, then cover and allow to stand for 5 minutes. Fluff up the grains with a fork, raking out any lumps, then stir the butter through. Add the currants, orange zest, orange juice, pistachios, parmesan and basil, then season with salt and freshly ground black pepper and mix well.

3 **To prepare the tomatoes,** cut about 1 cm (½ inch) off the tops to use as caps. Scoop out the seeds and pulp, and reserve for another use (see Note).

4 **Carefully spoon** the couscous stuffing into each tomato shell.

5 **Sit the tomatoes** in a roasting tin, transfer to the barbecue, then lower the lid and cook for 15 minutes. Replace the tomato caps and cook for another 5 minutes, or until tender.

6 **Remove from heat** and serve immediately.

Note: The tomato seeds and pulp can be chopped up and added to soups, risottos and tomato-based pasta sauces.

WILD RICE WITH PUMPKIN

SERVES 4–6

190 g (6¾ oz/1 cup) wild rice, rinsed

300 g (10½ oz) jap (kent) pumpkin, skin on, cut into 1 x 6 cm (½ x 2½ inch) wedges

400 g (14 oz) tin chickpeas, drained and rinsed

8 spring onions (scallions), finely sliced

50 g (1¾ oz/⅓ cup) currants

70 g (2½ oz/½ cup) pistachio nuts, roughly chopped

1 teaspoon garam masala

3 tablespoons pepitas (pumpkin seeds)

2 tablespoons pistachio oil or olive oil

2 teaspoons finely grated orange zest

1 large handful coriander (cilantro) leaves

1 large handful mint, torn

1 Put the rice in a small saucepan over medium–high heat, add 625 ml (21½ fl oz/2½ cups) of water and cover with a lid. Bring to the boil, then reduce the heat to low and simmer for 30–35 minutes, or until all of the liquid has been absorbed and the rice is cooked but still *al dente*.

2 Line a steamer with baking paper and punch with holes. Arrange the pumpkin on top and cover with a lid. Sit the steamer over a saucepan or wok of boiling water and steam for 5 minutes, or until the pumpkin is tender when pierced with a sharp knife. Set aside to cool a little.

3 Put the chickpeas, spring onion, currants, pistachios, garam masala, pepitas, oil, orange zest, coriander and mint leaves in a large bowl and season with salt and freshly ground black pepper.

4 Add the steamed rice and pumpkin wedges and toss gently to combine. Arrange in a bowl or on a platter and serve warm.

CARAMELIZED ONIONS AND LENTILS WITH SPINACH

SERVES 6

225 g (8 oz/1¼ cups) puy lentils or tiny blue-green lentils

3 tablespoons olive oil

2 red onions, finely sliced

2 garlic cloves, finely chopped

1 teaspoon ground coriander

1 teaspoon ground cumin

550 g (1 lb 4 oz) English spinach, rinsed well and stems trimmed

1 tablespoon lemon juice

2 tablespoons chopped coriander (cilantro) leaves

1 Put the lentils in a small saucepan over high heat, add 625 ml (21½ fl oz/2½ cups) of water and cover with a fitted lid. Bring to the boil, then reduce the heat to very low and simmer the lentils for 35 minutes, or until all of the water has been absorbed and the lentils are tender.

2 Meanwhile, heat the oil in a frying pan over medium heat and cook the onion, stirring occasionally, for 20 minutes, or until soft and caramelized. Add the garlic, ground coriander and cumin, season with salt and freshly ground black pepper and cook for a further 3 minutes. Remove from the heat.

3 Put the spinach in a large steamer and cover with a lid. Sit the steamer over a saucepan or wok of boiling water and steam for 3–5 minutes, or until wilted.

4 Combine the lentils, onion mixture and spinach in a large bowl, add the lemon juice and coriander and toss well.

SALADS

BROAD BEAN, FETA AND PRESERVED LEMON SALAD

SERVES 4

350 g (12 oz/2¼ cups) frozen broad (fava) beans

1 red capsicum (pepper), finely sliced

100 g (3½ oz) firm feta cheese, cut into cubes

1 tablespoon za'atar (see Note)

¼ small red onion, finely sliced

125 g (4½ oz) yellow baby tomatoes, cut in half

¼ preserved lemon, pulp removed, washed and finely sliced

100 g (3½ oz) mixed salad leaves

ORANGE DRESSING

2 teaspoons grated orange zest

2 tablespoons orange juice

2 tablespoons olive oil

1 teaspoon honey

1 teaspoon za'atar

1   Bring a saucepan of water to the boil. Add the broad beans and bring back to the boil. Cook for 5 minutes, drain, refresh under cold running water and peel the outer skins from the beans.

2   **Meanwhile,** in another small saucepan, blanch the red capsicum in boiling water for 1 minute, then drain, refresh and drain again. Sprinkle the feta cubes with the za'atar to coat on all sides. Combine all the dressing ingredients.

3   **Put the broad beans,** capsicum, onion and tomatoes in a large bowl. Add the preserved lemon. Pour over the dressing and toss. Add the feta cubes and toss gently. Put the salad leaves on serving plates and pile the combined mixture on top.

Note: Za'atar is a mixture of herbs and spices used as a condiment with Middle Eastern origins. The name of the condiment shares the Arabic name of the herb used as the main ingredient. It is generally prepared using ground dried thyme, oregano, marjoram, or some combination thereof, mixed with toasted sesame seeds, and salt. Some varieties may add savory, cumin, coriander or fennel seed.

BARBECUED POTATO SALAD WITH SALSA VERDE DRESSING

SERVES 4

1 kg (2 lb 4 oz) evenly sized kipfler
(fingerling) potatoes, scrubbed
and peeled

3 tablespoons olive oil

2 garlic cloves, crushed

SALSA VERDE DRESSING

1 tablespoon chopped oregano leaves

1 large handful flat-leaf (Italian) parsley

4 tablespoons extra virgin olive oil

3 garlic cloves, crushed

2 tablespoons capers, drained and
rinsed

2 anchovy fillets, drained

1 tablespoon lemon juice

1 **Preheat a kettle** or covered barbecue to medium heat.

2 **Cut the potatoes** in half on the diagonal. Toss them in a bowl with the oil and garlic and spread them on the barbecue grill. Lower the lid and cook the potatoes for 5 minutes on each side, or until cooked through — the exact cooking time will depend on the size of your potatoes.

3 **While the potatoes are cooking,** put the salsa verde dressing ingredients in a food processor and blend until smooth. Season to taste with salt and freshly ground black pepper.

4 **Put the potatoes** in a serving bowl and toss the salsa verde through. Serve warm.

EGGPLANT, TAHINI AND MINT SALAD

SERVES 4

TAHINI DRESSING
3 tablespoons tahini
2 teaspoons olive oil
1 garlic clove, crushed
2 tablespoons lemon juice

1 large eggplant (aubergine), thinly
   sliced
2 tablespoons olive oil
1 garlic clove, crushed
1 large handful mint leaves, roughly
   chopped
3 tablespoons chopped parsley
2 tablespoons thick plain yoghurt
¼ teaspoon mild smoky paprika

1 **To make the tahini dressing,** put all the ingredients in a food processor with 125 ml (4 fl oz/½ cup) of warm water. Blend until well combined and set aside until needed.

2 **Preheat a barbecue grill plate,** flat plate or chargrill pan to medium.

3 **Put the eggplant** slices in a large bowl, add the oil and garlic, then toss well to coat.

4 **Cook the eggplant** for about 3 minutes, or until grill marks appear, turning once. Place in a large bowl and allow to cool.

5 **Toss the mint,** parsley and tahini dressing through the eggplant slices, mixing well.

6 **Serve** at room temperature, generously topped with yoghurt and sprinkled with the paprika.

CARROT AND ALMOND SALAD

SERVES 4

4 large carrots

2 tablespoons peanut oil

1 teaspoon caster (superfine) sugar

½ teaspoon brown mustard seeds

¼ teaspoon curry powder

2 tablespoons lemon juice

25 g (1 oz/¼ cup) toasted flaked almonds

1 large handful coriander (cilantro) leaves

3 tablespoons thick plain yoghurt

1   Heat the grill (broiler) to medium.

2   Slice the carrots thinly, on the diagonal.

3   Put 1 tablespoon of the oil in a bowl, mix in the sugar, then add the carrot and toss to coat. Spread the carrot on a baking tray and grill for 10–15 minutes, turning occasionally, until lightly browned and tender. Remove from the heat and leave to cool, then place in a bowl.

4   While the carrots are grilling, heat the remaining oil in a small frying pan. Add the mustard seeds and curry powder and cook over low heat for 1 minute, or until fragrant. Allow to cool a little, then whisk in the lemon juice and season to taste.

5   Drizzle the spice mixture over the carrots, add the almonds and coriander and toss gently until well combined.

6   Serve at room temperature, with a dollop of yoghurt.

FATTOUSH SALAD

SERVES 4

1 Lebanese (large pitta) bread, split

2 baby cos (romaine) lettuces, torn into bite-sized pieces

2 tomatoes, chopped

2 small Lebanese (short) cucumbers, chopped

1 green capsicum (pepper), cut into large dice

4 spring onions (scallions), chopped

1 large handful mint, roughly chopped

1 large handful coriander (cilantro) leaves, roughly chopped

DRESSING

3 tablespoons lemon juice

3 tablespoons olive oil

1 tablespoon sumac

1 **Preheat the oven** to 180°C (350°F/Gas 4). Place the Lebanese bread on a baking tray and bake for 5 minutes, or until golden and crisp. Remove from the oven and cool. Break into 2 cm (¾ inch) pieces.

2 **To make the dressing,** mix the lemon juice, oil and sumac together and season to taste.

3 **In a serving bowl,** toss the lettuce, tomatoes, cucumbers, capsicum, spring onions and herbs together. Crumble over the toasted Lebanese bread, drizzle with the dressing and serve immediately.

Note: Sumac is a purple-red spice with a mild lemony flavour available from Middle Eastern grocery stores and gourmet food shops. If you can't obtain any, you could use ½ teaspoon sweet paprika in this recipe instead.

VEGETABLE SALAD WITH SHICHIMI TOGARASHI

SERVES 4

2 carrots, peeled and cut into matchsticks

2 celery stalks, cut into matchsticks

200 g (7 oz/2 cups) snow peas (mangetout), trimmed and cut into fine slices lengthways

1 small red capsicum (pepper), seeded and finely sliced

2 spring onions (scallions), cut diagonally into fine slices

150 g (5½ oz/1 ⅔ cups) bean sprouts, trimmed

6 radishes, finely sliced

1 tablespoon shichimi togarashi (see Note), for sprinkling

DRESSING

1 tablespoon rice vinegar

1 tablespoon mirin

1 tablespoon vegetable oil

2 teaspoons fish sauce **or light soy sauce**

1 teaspoon honey

1 **Bring a saucepan of water** to the boil. Add the carrots, celery, snow peas and capsicum. Bring back to the boil. Cook for 1 minute, then drain and refresh under cold running water and drain again.

2 **Put the blanched vegetables** in a large bowl. Add the spring onions, bean sprouts, and radishes. Combine the dressing ingredients, pour over the vegetables and toss well.

3 **Pile the salad** onto a serving platter and sprinkle with the shichimi togarashi.

Note: Shichimi togarashi is a Japanese spice mix containing seven different flavours. It always includes togarashi, a hot red Japanese chilli. The remaining ingredients are flexible but often include mustard, sesame seeds, poppy seeds, sansho, shiso or nori flakes. It is mainly used as a garnish.

POTATO, SPINACH, WHITE BEAN AND AVOCADO SALAD

SERVES 4–6

6 desiree or other all-purpose potatoes, washed

2 red capsicums (peppers), halved and seeded

100 g (3½ oz/1 cup) snow peas (mangetout), trimmed

3 tablespoons extra virgin olive oil

2 garlic cloves, finely chopped

1 teaspoon fish sauce or light soy sauce

1 teaspoon grated palm sugar (jaggery) or soft brown sugar

125 ml (4 fl oz/½ cup) lime juice

400 g (14 oz) tin cannellini beans, drained and rinsed

50 g (1¾ oz/1 cup) baby English spinach

1 large handful coriander (cilantro) leaves

2 avocados, diced

1 French shallot, finely chopped

1 small red chilli, seeded and finely chopped

1 **Line a double steamer** with baking paper and punch with holes. Lay the potatoes in the bottom tray and the capsicum in the top. Cover with a lid. Sit the steamer over a saucepan or wok of boiling water and steam for 30 minutes, or until the potatoes are tender. Put the capsicum in a plastic bag to cool, then peel and slice into strips.

2 **Lightly steam** the snow peas for 1–2 minutes, then slice into strips.

3 **Meanwhile,** peel the potatoes while they are still hot and cut into 1 cm (½ inch) rounds.

4 **Combine the oil,** garlic, fish sauce (or light soy sauce), sugar and 3 tablespoons of the lime juice in a bowl.

5 **Put the potato rounds** in a bowl and pour on half the dressing.

6 **Put the capsicum,** snow peas, cannellini beans, spinach and coriander in a large bowl. Pour on the remaining dressing and toss to combine.

7 **In a separate bowl** combine the avocado, shallot, chilli and remaining lime juice.

8 **To serve,** divide the potato slices among serving plates. Pile the bean salad over the potatoes and top with a good dollop of the avocado mixture.

FRESH BEETROOT AND BLUE CHEESE SALAD

SERVES 4

1 tablespoon olive oil

50 g (1¾ oz/½ cup) pecans

1.3 kg (3 lb) baby beetroot (beets),
washed, trimmed and halved

250 g (9 oz) baby green beans, trimmed

120 g (4¼ oz/4 cups) watercress,
trimmed

2 tablespoons walnut oil

1 teaspoon honey

2 teaspoons grated orange zest

1 tablespoon cider vinegar

50 g (1¾ oz) firm blue cheese,
finely sliced

1 Heat the oil in a frying pan over medium–high heat. Add the pecans and toast for 3 minutes, then sprinkle with salt and freshly ground black pepper. Remove from the heat and pour into a bowl lined with paper towels. Drain.

2 Line a large steamer with baking paper and punch with holes. Put the beetroot halves on top and cover with a lid. Sit the steamer over a saucepan or wok of boiling water and steam for 30–35 minutes, or until the beetroot is tender when pierced with a knife. Remove from the steamer and allow to cool.

3 Remove the baking paper from the steamer and add the baby beans. Cover and steam for 5–7 minutes, or until just tender. Remove and refresh under cold water.

4 Peel the skins from the beetroot and trim off any excess stem.

5 Put the pecans, beans and watercress in a large bowl and combine.

6 Combine the walnut oil, honey, orange zest and vinegar in a bowl, then pour over the salad. Carefully fold in the beetroot. Season to taste. Transfer to a serving platter and sprinkle blue cheese over the top.

CHICKPEA AND ROAST VEGETABLE SALAD

SERVES 8

500 g (1 lb) butternut pumpkin (squash), cubed

2 red capsicums (peppers), halved

4 slender eggplants (aubergines), cut in half lengthways

4 zucchini (courgettes), cut in half lengthways

4 onions, quartered

olive oil, for brushing

2 x 300 g (10 oz) cans chickpeas, rinsed and drained

2 tablespoons chopped fresh flat-leaf (Italian) parsley

DRESSING

80 ml (3 fl oz/⅓ cup) olive oil

2 tablespoons lemon juice

1 clove garlic, crushed

1 tablespoon chopped fresh thyme

1   **Preheat the oven** to hot 220°C (425°F/Gas 7). Brush two baking trays with oil and lay out the vegetables in a single layer. Brush lightly with oil.

2   **Bake for 40 minutes,** or until the vegetables are tender and begin to brown slightly on the edges. Cool.

3   **Remove the skins** from the capsicum if you want. Chop the capsicum, eggplant and zucchini into pieces, then put the vegetables in a bowl with the chickpeas and half the parsley.

4   **To make the dressing,** whisk together all the ingredients. Season, then toss with the vegetables. Leave for 30 minutes, then sprinkle with the rest of the parsley.

BEAN AND VEGETABLE SALAD WITH CHILLI AND VINEGAR

SERVES 4

2 fennel bulbs, trimmed and sliced lengthways

125 g (4½ oz/⅔ cup) baby corn, halved on the diagonal

150 g (5½ oz/1½ cups) snow peas (mangetout), trimmed and halved on the diagonal

400 g (14 oz) tin pinto or borlotti (cranberry) beans, drained and rinsed

100 g (3½ oz/4 cups) baby rocket (arugula)

40 g (1½ oz/1 heaped cup) snow pea (mangetout) sprouts

BLACK VINEGAR DRESSING

4 tablespoons olive oil

3 tablespoons black vinegar (see Note)

1 tablespoon rice vinegar

2 tablespoons finely chopped coriander (cilantro) leaves

1 small red chilli, seeded and finely chopped

1 **Line a steamer** with baking paper and punch with holes. Put the fennel and baby corn in the steamer and cover with a lid. Sit the steamer over a saucepan or wok of boiling water and steam for 5 minutes. Add the snow peas and beans and steam for a further 5 minutes. Transfer to a bowl, making sure you leave any condensed steaming liquid on the baking paper.

2 **Meanwhile,** to make the dressing, whisk together the oil, black vinegar and rice vinegar until well combined. Season well. Stir in the coriander and chilli.

3 **Pour half the dressing** over the vegetables, toss well, then leave for 5 minutes or to cool completely.

4 **To serve,** arrange the rocket leaves on a serving platter and drizzle with the remaining dressing. Spoon on the dressed vegetables and scatter the snow pea sprouts over the top.

Note: Black vinegar is similar to balsamic, but has a slightly smoky flavour. Buy it from Asian food stores or in the Asian section of larger supermarkets

ASPARAGUS AND MUSHROOM SALAD

SERVES 4

155 g (5 oz) asparagus spears

1 tablespoon wholegrain mustard

60 ml (2 fl oz/¼ cup) orange juice

2 tablespoons lemon juice

1 tablespoon lime juice

1 tablespoon orange zest

2 teaspoons lemon zest

2 teaspoons lime zest

2 cloves garlic, crushed

90 g (3 oz/¼ cup) honey

400 g (13 oz) button mushrooms, halved

150 g (5 oz) rocket (arugula)

1 red capsicum (pepper), cut into strips

1   Snap the woody ends from the asparagus spears and cut in half on the diagonal. Cook in boiling water for 1 minute, or until just tender. Drain, plunge into cold water and set aside.

2   Place the mustard, citrus juice and zest, garlic and honey in a large saucepan and season with freshly ground black pepper. Bring to the boil, then reduce the heat and add the mushrooms, tossing for 2 minutes. Cool.

3   Remove the mushrooms from the sauce with a slotted spoon. Return the sauce to the heat, bring to the boil, then reduce the heat and simmer for 3–5 minutes, or until reduced and syrupy. Cool slightly.

4   Toss the mushrooms, rocket leaves, capsicum and asparagus. Put on a plate and drizzle with the sauce.

HOKKIEN NOODLE SALAD

SERVES 8

900 g (1¾ lb) hokkien noodles

6 spring onions, sliced diagonally

1 large red capsicum (pepper), thinly sliced

200 g (7 oz) snow peas (mangetout), sliced

1 carrot, sliced diagonally

60 g (2 oz) fresh mint, chopped

60 g (2 oz) fresh coriander (cilantro), chopped

100 g (3½ oz) roasted cashew nuts

SESAME DRESSING

2 teaspoons sesame oil

1 tablespoon peanut oil

2 tablespoons lime juice

2 tablespoons kecap manis (see Note)

3 tablespoons sweet chilli sauce

1 **Gently separate** the noodles and place in a large bowl, cover with boiling water and leave 2 minutes. Rinse and drain.

2 **Put the noodles** in a large bowl, and add spring onions, capsicum, snow peas, carrot, mint and coriander. Toss together well.

3 **To make the dressing,** whisk together the oils, lime juice, kecap manis and sweet chilli sauce. Pour the dressing over the salad and toss again.

4 **Sprinkle the cashew nuts** over the top and serve immediately.

Note: If you can't find kecap manis, you can use soy sauce sweetened with a little soft brown sugar.

JAPANESE WHITE SALAD

SERVES 6–8

TOFU DRESSING

200 g (7 oz) silken firm tofu

50 g (1¾ oz/⅓ cup), sesame seeds, toasted

1 tablespoon caster (superfine) sugar

1½ tablespoon white miso paste

1½ tablespoon water

2 teaspoons shoyu (Japanese soy sauce)

3 teaspoons mirin

3 teaspoons sake

SALAD

100 g (3½ oz) konnyaku (yam cake)

1 small carrot, peeled

170 ml (5½ fl oz/⅔ cup) water

3 teaspoons shoyu (Japanese soy sauce)

1 tablespoon mirin

12 baby green beans, cut into 3 cm (1¼ inch) lengths

6 fresh shiitake mushrooms, stems discarded, caps sliced

1 **To weight the tofu,** first wrap it in a clean tea towel (dish towel). Put two plates on top of the tofu and leave for about 2 hours to extract any excess moisture.

2 **Meanwhile,** prepare the salad. Boil the konnyaku for 2 minutes, then cut into 3 cm x 5 mm (1¼ x ¼ in) strips. Cut the carrot into 5 cm (2 in) long pieces. Slice each piece into thin, 1 cm (½ in) wide batons.

3 **Combine the water,** shoyu and mirin in a saucepan and bring to the boil over high heat. Reduce to a simmer, then add the konnyaku, carrot and beans and cook for 3 minutes, or until the carrot is tender. Remove the vegetables with a slotted spoon and set aside. Add the shiitake to the pan, increase the heat to high and cook for 1–2 minutes, or until the liquid has almost evaporated. Cool completely.

4 **Remove the tofu from the tea towel,** then pat dry with paper towels. Finely mash the tofu with the back of a fork and set aside.

5 **To make the dressing,** grind the sesame seeds using a mortar and pestle until finely crushed. Gradually mix in the sugar, miso, water, shoyu, mirin and sake until smooth. Stir the mashed tofu into the mixture.

6 **Put the cooled carrot** and shiitake mixtures in a bowl with the dressing and toss to combine.

7 **Serve** in a neat mound in a large serving bowl or in small individual dishes.

CHARGRILLED CAULIFLOWER SALAD WITH TAHINI DRESSING

SERVES 4

TAHINI DRESSING

65 g (2¼ oz/¼ cup) tahini

1 garlic clove, crushed

60 ml (2 fl oz/¼ cup) seasoned rice
   vinegar

1 tablespoon vegetable oil

1 teaspoon lime juice

¼ teaspoon sesame oil

1 head of cauliflower

12 garlic cloves, crushed

2 tablespoons vegetable oil

2 baby cos (romaine) lettuces, leaves
   separated

50 g (1¾ oz/1⅔ cups) watercress sprigs

2 teaspoons sesame seeds, toasted

1 tablespoon chopped flat-leaf (Italian)
   parsley

1 **Heat a chargrill pan** or barbecue grill plate to medium.

2 **To make the tahini,** put all the ingredients in a non-metallic bowl with 1 tablespoon water. Whisk together well and season to taste with sea salt and freshly ground black pepper.

3 **Cut the cauliflower** in half, then into 1 cm (½ inch) wedges. Place on a tray and gently rub with the garlic and oil. Season well, then chargrill, in batches if necessary, until golden on both sides and cooked through. Remove from the heat.

4 **Arrange the lettuce** and watercress in a salad bowl and top with the cauliflower. Drizzle the dressing over the cauliflower, sprinkle with the sesame seeds and parsley and serve.

MEDITERRANEAN LENTIL SALAD

SERVES 4–6

1 large red capsicum (pepper)

1 large yellow capsicum (pepper)

250 g (9 oz/1 cup) red lentils

1 red onion, finely chopped

1 Lebanese (short) cucumber, chopped

DRESSING

80 ml (2½ fl oz/⅓ cup) olive oil

2 tablespoons lemon juice

1 teaspoon ground cumin

2 garlic cloves, crushed

1 **Cut the capsicums** into large flat pieces and remove the seeds and membranes. Cook, skin side up, under a hot grill (broiler) until the skins blister and blacken. Leave to cool in a plastic bag, then peel away the skin and cut the flesh into thin strips. Place in a salad bowl and set aside.

2 **Meanwhile,** cook the lentils in a saucepan of boiling water for 10 minutes, or until tender; do not overcook or they will become mushy. Drain well.

3 **Add the lentils** to the capsicum with the onion and cucumber. Toss to combine.

4 **To make the dressing,** put all the ingredients in a small bowl and whisk together. Season well with sea salt and freshly ground black pepper, pour over the salad and mix well.

5 **Cover and refrigerate** for 4 hours to allow the flavours to develop. Serve at room temperature.

SUMMER SALAD WITH MARINATED TOFU STEAKS

SERVES 4

500 g (1 lb 2 oz) block firm tofu

2 tablespoons balsamic vinegar

1 tablespoon olive oil

1 garlic clove, crushed

SUMMER SALAD

250 g (9 oz) cherry tomatoes, halved

½ red onion, thinly sliced

1 small Lebanese (short) cucumber, sliced

1 handful basil leaves, shredded

12 pitted kalamata olives, halved

2 teaspoons balsamic vinegar

2 teaspoons extra virgin olive oil

1 **Cut the tofu horizontally** into four thin steaks, or into four large cubes if you prefer. Place in a large, shallow non-metallic dish and drizzle with the vinegar and oil. Add the garlic and season well with salt and freshly ground black pepper. Use your fingers to rub the mixture evenly all over the tofu, then cover and refrigerate for at least 30 minutes, or up to 4 hours, turning occasionally.

2 **Preheat a barbecue** flat plate to moderately hot.

3 **When you're nearly ready** to eat, make the salad. Put the tomato, onion, cucumber, basil, olives and vinegar in a bowl, drizzle with the oil and toss together gently. Season well.

4 **Cook the tofu** on the hotplate for 2 minutes on each side, or until golden.

5 **Transfer to four** serving plates and pile the salad over the top. Serve with crusty bread.

MAINS

CHILLI AND TOFU STIR-FRY

SERVES 6

3 tablespoons peanut oil

1 teaspoon bottled crushed chilli

2 teaspoons grated fresh ginger

2 garlic cloves, crushed

250 g (9 oz) hard tofu, cut into
1.5 cm (⅝ inch) cubes

8 spring onions (scallions), sliced on
the diagonal

150 g (5½ oz/¾ cup) fresh baby corn,
halved lengthways

150 g (5½ oz/1½ cups) snowpeas
(mangetout), topped and tailed

500 g (1 lb 2 oz) hokkien (egg) noodles

40 g (1½ oz/¼ cup) cashew nuts

2 tablespoons soy sauce

125 ml (4 fl oz/½ cup) vegetable stock

1 handful coriander (cilantro) leaves

1 Heat the oil in a wok over medium heat and swirl to coat. Add the chilli, ginger and garlic and stir-fry for about 2–3 minutes, or until aromatic.

2 Add the tofu cubes, spring onion and baby corn and stir-fry for 2–3 minutes.

3 Add the snowpeas, noodles and cashews and cook, stirring, for 3–5 minutes, or until the vegetables are almost tender. Do not overcook.

4 Stir in the soy sauce and stock, then bring to the boil and simmer for 2 minutes, or until slightly reduced.

5 Stir in the coriander and serve immediately.

SMOKY SPICED EGGPLANT

SERVES 4

2 large (600 g/1 lb 5 oz) eggplants (aubergines)

1 red onion, chopped

1 garlic clove, chopped

2.5 cm (1 inch) piece of ginger, chopped

1 green chilli, chopped

100 ml (3½ fl oz) oil

¼ teaspoon chilli powder

½ teaspoon garam masala

2 teaspoons ground cumin

2 teaspoons ground coriander (cilantro)

2 teaspoons salt

½ teaspoon freshly ground black pepper

2 ripe tomatoes, chopped

3–4 tablespoons coriander (cilantro) leaves, finely chopped

1 **Using a pair of tongs,** scorch the eggplants by holding them over a medium gas flame. Alternatively, heat them under a grill (broiler) or on an electric hotplate. Keep turning them until the skin is blackened on all sides. Set aside until cool, then peel off the charred skin. Roughly chop the flesh. Don't worry if black specks remain on the flesh because they add to the smoky flavour.

2 **Combine the onion,** garlic, ginger and chilli in a blender and process until chopped together but not a paste. Alternatively, chop finely with a knife and mix in a bowl.

3 **Heat oil** in a deep heavy-based frying pan over medium heat, add the onion mixture and cook until slightly browned.

4 **Add all the spices** and the salt and pepper and stir for 1 minute. Add the tomato and simmer until liquid has reduced.

5 **Put the eggplants** in the pan and mash them with a wooden spoon, stirring around with the spices. Simmer for about 10 minutes, or until soft.

6 **Stir in the coriander leaves** and season with salt.

7 **Serve hot with bread** as a light meal, or refrigerate and serve as a cold relish with an Indian curry.

HARISSA WITH VEGETABLE COUSCOUS

SERVES 4

HARISSA

3 dried bird's eye chillies

3 large garlic cloves

1 teaspoon coriander seeds

½ teaspoon ground cumin

60 ml (2 fl oz/¼ cup) extra virgin
  olive oil

60 ml (2 fl oz/¼ cup) tomato passata
  (puréed tomatoes)

1 tablespoon tomato paste
  (concentrated purée)

2 tablespoons roughly chopped
  coriander (cilantro)

2 tablespoons roughly chopped mint

250 g (9 oz/1 cup) Greek-style yoghurt

300 g (10½ oz/1⅔ cups) couscous

60 ml (2 fl oz/¼ cup) olive oil

1 large onion, halved and thinly sliced

3 zucchini (courgettes), thinly sliced

2 large carrots, cut into fine matchsticks
  2 cm (¾ inch) long

400 g (14 oz) tin chickpeas, rinsed
  and drained

40 g (1½ oz/⅓ cup) sultanas
  (golden raisins)

30 g (1 oz/¼ cup) toasted slivered
  almonds

2 tablespoons baby capers, rinsed and
  squeezed dry

1 **To make the harissa,** put the chillies, garlic, coriander seeds and cumin in a mini processor. Whizz for 30 seconds, or until roughly ground. Add the olive oil, tomato passata and tomato paste and whizz for 12–15 seconds, or until smooth.

2 **Put the coriander,** mint and yoghurt in a small bowl and mix to combine.

3 **Prepare the couscous** according to the manufacturer's instructions. Cover and set aside.

4 **Heat the oil** in a large frying pan over medium heat. Add the onion and fry for 5–6 minutes, or until softened. Add the zucchini and carrot and fry for 5 minutes, or until just tender and beginning to brown. Stir in the chickpeas and sultanas. Add the couscous, stirring gently until well combined.

5 **Divide the couscous mixture** among four plates and sprinkle with the toasted almonds and capers. Serve with the harissa and herbed yoghurt, to taste.

SWEET AND SOUR CHICKPEAS

SERVES 4–6

500 g (2¼ cups) chickpeas

2 tablespoons oil or ghee

2 large red onions, thinly sliced

2 cm (¾ inch) piece of ginger, finely chopped

2 teaspoons sugar

2 teaspoons ground coriander (cilantro)

2 teaspoons ground cumin

pinch of chilli powder (optional)

1 teaspoon garam masala

3 tablespoons tamarind purée (see Note)

4 ripe tomatoes, chopped

4 tablespoons coriander (cilantro) or mint leaves, finely chopped

1 Put the chickpeas in a bowl, cover with water and leave overnight to rehydrate.

2 Drain the chickpeas, then put them in a large saucepan with 2 litres (8 cups) water. Bring to the boil, spooning off any scum from the surface. Cover and simmer over low heat for 1–1½ hours until soft. It is important they are soft at this stage as they won't soften any more once the sauce has been added. Drain.

3 Heat the oil in a heavy-based frying pan. Fry the onion until soft and brown, then stir in the ginger.

4 Add the chickpeas, sugar, coriander, cumin, chilli powder, garam masala and a pinch of salt. Stir, then add the tamarind and tomato and simmer for 2–3 minutes.

5 Add 500 ml (2 cups) water, bring to the boil and cook until the sauce has thickened. Stir in the coriander leaves.

6 Serve with Indian bread such as rotis or naan.

Note: Tamarind is a souring agent made from the pods of the tamarind tree. It is sold as a block of pulp (including husks and seeds), as cleaned pulp, or as ready-prepared tamarind purée or concentrate. It is available in Asian supermarkets.

PENNE WITH ZUCCHINI, RICOTTA AND PARMESAN SAUCE

SERVES 4

500 g (1 lb 2 oz/5½ cups) small
　penne pasta

PARMESAN SAUCE

2 zucchini (courgettes), chopped

2 garlic cloves, chopped

1 small red chilli, seeded and chopped

125 g (4½ oz/½ cup) ricotta cheese

100 ml (3½ fl oz) pouring cream

2 teaspoons finely grated lemon zest

100 g (3½ oz/1 cup) grated
　parmesan cheese

1 handful basil, chopped

small basil leaves, to serve

parmesan cheese shavings, to serve

1 **Cook the penne pasta** in a large saucepan of boiling salted water according to the manufacturer's instructions. Drain the penne, reserving 125 ml (4 fl oz/½ cup) of the cooking water.

2 **Meanwhile,** to make the sauce, put the zucchini, garlic and chilli in a small processor fitted with the metal blade and whizz in short bursts for 30 seconds, or until finely chopped. Add the ricotta, cream, lemon zest, parmesan and chopped basil, and season well with salt and freshly ground black pepper. Whizz for 20 seconds, or until smooth.

3 **Pour the sauce** over the hot penne, adding enough of the reserved cooking water to make a coating consistency.

4 **Serve immediately,** topped with basil leaves and parmesan shavings.

Note: Prepare the sauce just prior to serving. It is not suitable for freezing.

GREAT TASTES VEGETARIAN

CHU CHEE TOFU

SERVES 6

CURRY PASTE

10 small fresh red chillies

50 g (1¾ oz) red Asian shallots, peeled

1 tablespoon finely chopped coriander (cilantro) stem and root

1 stem lemon grass (white part only), chopped

2 tablespoons grated fresh galangal

2 cloves garlic

1 tablespoon ground coriander (cilantro)

1 teaspoon ground cumin

1 teaspoon black peppercorns

½ teaspoon ground turmeric

1 tablespoon lime juice

1 tablespoon oil

1 onion, finely chopped

2 cups (500 ml/16 fl oz) coconut milk

200 g (6½ oz) fried tofu puffs, halved on the diagonal

fresh coriander (cilantro) sprigs, to garnish

1 To make the curry paste, place all the ingredients in a food processor or spice grinder and process until smooth.

2 Heat the oil in a large saucepan, add the onion and cook over medium heat for 4–5 minutes, or until starting to brown. Add 3 tablespoons of the curry paste and cook, stirring, for 2 minutes.

3 Stir in the coconut milk and ½ cup (125 ml/4 fl oz) water, and season with salt. Bring slowly to the boil, stirring constantly.

4 Add the tofu puffs, then reduce the heat and simmer, stirring frequently, for 5 minutes, or until the sauce thickens slightly. Garnish with fresh coriander sprigs and serve with steamed rice.

CHEESE TORTELLINI WITH PISTACHIO AND LIME SAUCE

SERVES 4

3 slices white bread, crusts removed

100 g (3½ oz/⅔ cup) pistachio kernels

grated zest of 1 lime

1 garlic clove, chopped

50 g (1¾ oz/½ cup) grated
  parmesan cheese

1 handful flat-leaf (Italian) parsley

2 teaspoons thyme

80 ml (2½ fl oz/⅓ cup) olive oil

500 g (1 lb 2 oz) cheese tortellini

grated parmesan cheese, to serve

1   Put the bread in a mini processor and whizz for
30 seconds, or until breadcrumbs form. Remove half of the
crumbs and set aside.

2   Add the pistachios, lime zest, garlic, parmesan, parsley and
thyme to the processor containing the remaining crumbs and
whizz for 30 seconds, or until the mixture forms a coarse paste.
With the motor running, gradually add 60 ml (2 fl oz/¼ cup) of
the oil. Season well with salt and freshly ground black pepper.

3   Cook the cheese tortellini in a large saucepan of boiling
salted water according to the manufacturer's instructions.
Drain the tortellini, reserving 250 ml (9 fl oz/1 cup) of the
cooking water.

4   Meanwhile, heat the remaining oil in a small frying pan
over medium heat. Add the reserved breadcrumbs and stir
for 1–2 minutes, or until lightly golden.

5   Stir the sauce through the hot tortellini, adding enough
of the reserved cooking water to make a coating consistency.

6   Serve immediately, topped with the toasted breadcrumbs
and grated parmesan.

COUSCOUS WITH GRILLED FENNEL

SERVES 4

4 baby fennel bulbs, with fronds

olive oil, for brushing

2 red onions, each cut into 8 wedges

250 ml (9 fl oz/1 cup) vegetable stock

140 g (5 oz/¾ cup) couscous

PRESERVED LEMON DRESSING

1 preserved lemon quarter

4 tablespoons virgin olive oil

½ teaspoon dijon mustard

1½ tablespoons lemon juice

1 **Bring a saucepan** of water to the boil.

2 **Meanwhile,** trim the fronds from the fennel bulbs. Chop up enough fronds to fill a tablespoon and reserve for the couscous. Remove the stalks from the fennel and cut a 5 mm (¼ inch) thick slice off the base of each bulb. Cut the bulbs into quarters, then add them to the pan of boiling water. Cook, covered, for about 3 minutes, or until tender. Drain well.

3 **Heat the grill** (broiler) to medium. Lightly brush the grill tray with oil and spread the fennel and onion wedges over the top, taking care not to crowd them. Brush the vegetables with a little olive oil and grill for 10 minutes, or until tender and lightly coloured, turning the vegetables during cooking.

4 **While the vegetables are grilling,** make the preserved lemon dressing. Scoop out and discard the flesh from the preserved lemon. Wash the rind thoroughly, then pat dry and finely chop. In a small bowl, whisk the oil, mustard and lemon juice together until combined. Add the preserved lemon and season to taste.

5 **To prepare the couscous,** bring the stock to the boil in a saucepan. Stir in the couscous and reserved chopped fennel leaves and take the pan off the heat. Cover and leave for 4–5 minutes, then fluff up the couscous with a fork, raking out any lumps.

6 **Transfer the couscous** to a serving dish and arrange the grilled fennel and onion wedges over the top. Drizzle the dressing over the top and serve.

CHIANG MAI VEGETABLE CURRY

SERVES 4

2 dried red chillies

2 teaspoons coriander seeds

5 cm (2 inch) piece galangal or ginger, finely chopped

10 cm (4 inch) piece lemongrass, chopped

4 red Asian shallots, finely chopped

1 teaspoon ground cumin

½ teaspoon ground cinnamon

3 garlic cloves, crushed

5 cm (2 inch) piece fresh ginger, finely grated

2 tablespoons vegetable oil

½ teaspoon ground turmeric

3 tablespoons coconut milk

200 g (7 oz) fresh shiitake mushrooms, roughly chopped

125 g (4½ oz/1 cup) green beans, cut into 5 cm (2 inch) pieces

125 g (4½ oz/⅔ cup, heaped) baby corn, halved on the diagonal

1 tablespoon lemon juice

1 tablespoon soy sauce

2 teaspoons sugar

2 tablespoons fish sauce or light soy sauce

65 g (2¼ oz/¾ cup) bean sprouts, tails trimmed

coriander (cilantro) leaves, to serve

1 **Soak the dried chillies** in hot water for 10 minutes, then drain and roughly chop.

2 **Put the chopped chilli,** coriander seeds, galangal, lemon grass, shallots, cumin and cinnamon in a small food processor and grind to a paste, or pound with a mortar and pestle. If it seems too dry, add 1 tablespoon of water.

3 **In a separate bowl** combine the garlic and ginger.

4 **Heat the oil** in a wok over medium heat and cook the garlic and ginger paste for about 30 seconds. Add the curry paste and cook for 2 minutes, or until aromatic.

5 **Add one by one,** stirring well after each addition, the ground turmeric, coconut milk, mushrooms, beans, baby corn, lemon juice, soy sauce, sugar, fish sauce (or light soy sauce) and 250 ml (9 fl oz/1 cup) of boiling water. Cook for 2 minutes.

6 **Serve,** garnished with the bean sprouts and coriander leaves. Serve with noodles or rice.

RISI E BISI

SERVES 4

1.5 litres (52 fl oz/6 cups) chicken stock
2 teaspoons olive oil
40 g (1½ oz) butter
1 small onion, finely chopped
2 tablespoons chopped parsley
350 g (12 oz/2½ cups) shelled young peas
200 g (7 oz) risotto rice (arborio, vialone nano or carnaroli)
50 g (2 oz/½ cup) grated Parmesan cheese

1 **Put the stock** in a saucepan, bring to the boil and then maintain at a low simmer.

2 **Heat the oil** and half the butter in a large wide heavy-based saucepan and cook the onion over low heat for 5 minutes until softened. Stir in the parsley and peas and add 2 ladlefuls of the stock. Simmer for 6–8 minutes.

3 **Add the rice** and the remaining stock. Simmer until the rice is al dente and most of the stock has been absorbed. Stir in the remaining butter and the Parmesan, season with salt and freshly ground black pepper.

PUY LENTILS AND BEAN PUREE ON MUSHROOMS

SERVES 4

24 large (10 cm/4 inch) field mushrooms, stalks removed and sliced

1 tablespoon olive oil

1 red onion, cut into thin wedges

1 clove garlic, crushed

200 g (6½ oz/1 cup) puy lentils

185 ml (6 fl oz/¾ cup) red wine

440 ml (14 fl oz/2 cups) vegetable stock

1 tablespoon finely chopped fresh flat-leaf parsley

30 g (1 oz) butter

2 cloves garlic, crushed, extra

BEAN PUREE

1 large potato, cut into chunks

2 tablespoons extra virgin olive oil

400 g (13 oz) can cannellini beans, drained and rinsed

2 large garlic cloves, crushed

1 tablespoon vegetable stock

RED WINE SAUCE

170 ml (5½ fl oz/⅔ cup) red wine

2 tablespoons tomato paste (purée)

375 ml (12 fl oz/1½ cups) vegetable stock

1 tablespoon soft brown sugar

1 Heat the oil in a large saucepan and cook the onion over medium heat for 2–3 minutes, or until soft. Add the garlic and mushroom stalks and cook for a further 1 minute. Stir in the lentils, wine and stock and bring to the boil. Reduce the heat and simmer, covered, for 20–25 minutes, stirring occasionally, or until reduced and the lentils are cooked through. If the mixture is too wet, remove the lid and boil until slightly thick. Stir in the parsley and keep warm.

2 Meanwhile, to make the bean purée, bring a small saucepan of water to the boil over high heat and cook the potato for 10 minutes, or until tender. Drain and mash with a potato masher or fork until smooth. Stir in half the extra virgin olive oil. Combine the cannellini beans and garlic in a food processor bowl. Add the stock and the remaining oil and process until smooth. Transfer to a bowl and fold in the mashed potato. Keep warm.

3 Melt the butter in a deep frying pan. Add the mushrooms and extra garlic and cook in batches over medium heat for 4 minutes each side, or until tender. Remove and keep warm (do not put them in a hot oven or they will shrivel).

4 To make the red wine sauce, add the red wine to the same frying pan, then scrape the bottom to remove any sediment. Add the combined tomato paste, stock and sugar and bring to the boil. Cook for about 10 minutes, or until reduced and thickened.

5 To assemble, place the mushrooms onto serving plates and top with the bean purée. Spoon on the lentil mixture and drizzle with the red wine sauce. Season and serve immediately.

OPEN LASAGNE WITH ROCKET AND WALNUT PESTO

SERVES 4

PESTO

100 g (3½ oz/1 cup) walnuts

2 garlic cloves

2 large handfuls baby rocket (arugula)

1 large handful basil

1 large handful flat-leaf (Italian) parsley

100 ml (3½ fl oz) extra virgin olive oil

80 ml (2½ fl oz/⅓ cup) walnut oil

50 g (1¾ oz/½ cup) grated pecorino cheese

100 g (3½ oz/1 cup) grated parmesan cheese

375 g (13 oz) fresh lasagne sheets

1 tablespoon olive oil

4 large handfuls baby English spinach

1 garlic clove, sliced

2 tablespoons lemon juice

200 g (7 oz) marinated goat's feta cheese, crumbled

2 tablespoons grated parmesan cheese

1 To make the pesto, preheat the oven to 180°C (350°F/ Gas 4). Rinse the walnuts in cold water, then shake dry. Spread the walnuts on a baking tray and bake for 5–8 minutes, or until lightly golden. Watch carefully as they will burn easily. Transfer the walnuts to a small processor fitted with the metal blade. Add the garlic, rocket, basil and parsley and whizz in 3-second bursts for 1 minute, or until the mixture resembles coarse breadcrumbs. With the motor running, add the oils in a thin stream, then add the pecorino and parmesan and whizz for 40 seconds. Cover with plastic wrap and set aside.

2 Cut the lasagne sheets into sixteen 8 cm (3¼ inch) squares. Cook a few squares at a time in a large saucepan of boiling salted water for 4 minutes, or until *al dente*. Lay them on a clean tea towel (dish towel) and cover to keep warm while the remaining squares are cooked.

3 Heat the olive oil in a large frying pan over medium heat, add the spinach and garlic and sauté until just wilted. Add the lemon juice and stir to combine. Cover and keep warm

4 To serve, spoon 1 tablespoon of the pesto onto four warmed plates and spread out with the back of the spoon to the size of one of the pasta squares. Cover with a pasta square, then divide one-third of the spinach over the pasta. Sprinkle with one-third of the goat's feta, cover with another pasta square and spread with the pesto. Repeat the layers, finishing with a layer of pesto. Sprinkle with the grated parmesan and serve immediately.

Note: Store the pesto, covered with a thin layer of olive oil in an airtight container, in the refrigerator for up to 3 days.

GRILLED ASPARAGUS AND ZUCCHINI LASAGNE

SERVES 4

500 g (1 lb 2 oz) asparagus spears, trimmed

500 g (1 lb 2 oz) zucchini (courgettes), sliced lengthways into 5 mm (¼ inch) thick ribbons

2 tablespoons olive oil

6 large (20 x 15 cm/8 x 6 inch) fresh lasagne sheets

150 g (5½ oz/1 cup) grated mozzarella cheese

WHITE SAUCE

500 ml (17 fl oz/2 cups) milk

50 g (1¾ oz) butter

50 g (1¾ oz) plain (all-purpose) flour

125 ml (4 fl oz/½ cup) thick (double/heavy) cream

pinch of grated nutmeg

1 Heat the grill (broiler) to medium. Put the asparagus and zucchini in a large bowl, add the oil and gently toss to coat. Spread on a large baking tray and grill in batches for 2–3 minutes, or until lightly chargrilled and cooked, turning during cooking. Remove and leave to cool a little, then cut the asparagus into shorter lengths.

2 Bring a large saucepan of water to the boil. Add some salt and bring to the boil again. Add the lasagne sheets and stir gently with a wooden spoon. Boil for about 5–7 minutes, or until the water boils again and the pasta is *al dente* (the cooking time will vary according to the thickness of your lasagne sheets). Drain into a large colander, then carefully lay the sheets on a clean tea towel (dish towel) to dry.

3 Preheat the oven to 180°C (350°F/Gas 4).

4 Meanwhile, make the white sauce. Gently heat the milk in a small saucepan and set aside. In another saucepan, melt the butter and stir in the flour. Cook over medium heat, stirring with a wooden spoon, for about 3 minutes. Gradually add the milk and stir for 5 minutes, or until the sauce becomes smooth and boils and thickens. Remove from the heat and stir through the cream and nutmeg. Season with salt and white pepper to taste.

5 Lay 2 pasta sheets in a lightly oiled 20 x 30 cm (8 x 12 inch) baking dish and trim off any excess. Pour a little white sauce over the top and spread it about evenly. Arrange a layer of grilled vegetables on top, then spread with some more of the white sauce. Repeat to form another two layers, then scatter the grated mozzarella over the top. Bake for 45 minutes, or until the cheese is golden brown.

EGGPLANT ROLLS

SERVES 4

TOMATO SAUCE

2 tablespoons olive oil

1 small onion, finely diced

1 celery stalk, finely diced

½ small leek, finely diced

2 garlic cloves, crushed

4 tablespoons red wine

400 g (14 oz) tin chopped tomato

1 tablespoon tomato paste
   (concentrated purée)

½ teaspoon finely chopped
   thyme leaves

½ teaspoon finely chopped
   oregano leaves

1 teaspoon soft brown sugar

2 large eggplants (aubergines)

3 tablespoons olive oil

250 g (9 oz/1 cup) ricotta cheese

2 large handfuls basil leaves, finely
   shredded

75 g (2½ oz/½ cup) grated mozzarella
   cheese

1 **First,** make the tomato sauce. Heat the oil in a saucepan, add the onion, celery and leek and cook, stirring, over medium heat for 5 minutes, or until they start to soften. Add the garlic and cook for another 1–2 minutes, or until the garlic starts to turn golden. Pour in the wine and cook for 4 minutes, or until it has almost evaporated. Stir in the tomato, tomato paste and herbs, then simmer over low heat, stirring frequently, for 15–20 minutes, or until the sauce has thickened. Stir in the sugar and add some salt and freshly ground black pepper to taste. Cover and keep warm until needed.

2 **While the sauce is simmering,** heat a chargrill pan to medium. Cut each eggplant lengthways into six evenly sized slices about 1 cm (½ inch) thick, discarding the end pieces or reserving them for another recipe. Lightly brush each slice with the oil. Working in batches, chargrill the eggplant slices for

1–2 minutes, then rotate them at right angles and cook for another 1–2 minutes to get a crisscross chargrill pattern underneath. Flip the slices over and repeat on the other side. Repeat with the remaining eggplant.

3 **Heat the grill** (broiler) to its highest setting. Put the ricotta in a bowl with two-thirds of the basil and mix until smooth. Season with salt and freshly ground black pepper. Spread ricotta mixture evenly over each eggplant slice, then roll the slices up from one end and place seam side down in a shallow 18 x 22 cm (7 x 8½ inch) ovenproof dish. Spoon warm tomato sauce over the top and sprinkle with the grated mozzarella.

4 **Put the dish** under the hot grill and cook the rolls for 7 minutes, or until the cheese is golden and bubbling. Serve on a bed of freshly cooked egg fettucine, scattered with the remaining basil.

CREPES WITH PUMPKIN, GOAT'S CHEESE AND SAGE

SERVES 4

CREPE BATTER

310 ml (10¾ fl oz/1¼ cups) milk

50 g (1¾ oz) butter

155 g (5½ oz/1¼ cups) plain
    (all-purpose) flour

3 eggs

melted butter, for pan-frying

FILLING

400 g (14 oz) butternut pumpkin
    (squash), peeled

2 tablespoons olive oil

125 ml (4 fl oz/½ cup) vegetable oil

30 g (1 oz/1 bunch) sage, leaves plucked

250 g (9 oz) soft goat's cheese

TOPPING

300 ml (10½ fl oz) thick (double/heavy)
    cream

150 g (5½ oz) fontina cheese, grated

1 To make the crepe batter, gently heat the milk and butter in a small saucepan until the butter has melted, but do not allow the milk to boil. Put the flour and a good pinch of salt in a large bowl and make a well in the centre. Add the eggs and slowly whisk in the warm milk mixture. Whisk until the mixture is smooth and thin. Cover and leave to stand for 10–15 minutes.

2 Put a non-stick frying pan over medium heat. When hot, drizzle melted butter over the base. Add 60 ml (2 fl oz/¼ cup) of the batter and swirl to cover the base. Cook for 30 seconds, or until the crepe is set and bubbles start to appear. Using a spatula, turn the crepe over and cook for another 30 seconds. Remove to a plate and repeat until you have 12 perfect crepes.

3 Heat a chargrill pan to medium. Cut the pumpkin into 24 slices, each about 1 cm (½ inch) thick. Put them in a large bowl with the olive oil and toss with freshly ground black

pepper to coat. Chargrill the pumpkin in batches for 2 minutes, or until cooked through, turning once. Set aside to cool.

4 Put the vegetable oil in a small frying pan. Heat until the oil starts to haze — but do not let it burn. Quickly fry the sage leaves in batches until crisp, then remove and drain.

5 Heat the oven grill (broiler) to its highest setting. Put 2 pumpkin slices, some goat's cheese and a few sage leaves in one quarter of each crepe, saving some sage leaves for the garnish. Fold the crepes up into neat triangles and divide among four ovenproof oval gratin dishes or shallow pasta dishes.

6 To make the topping, heat the cream in a small saucepan, then stir in the grated cheese. Pour the mixture evenly over the crepes. Sit the dishes on a large baking tray, put the tray under the grill and cook for 3–5 minutes, or until the cheese is bubbling and hot. Scatter with reserved crispy sage leaves.

MUSHROOMS WITH TOFU

SERVES 2

350 g (12 oz) firm tofu (bean curd)

1 teaspoon sesame oil

2 teaspoons light soy sauce

¼ teaspoon ground black pepper, plus some to sprinkle

1 tablespoon finely shredded ginger

5 tablespoons vegetable stock or water

2 tablespoons light soy sauce

2 teaspoons cornflour (cornstarch)

½ teaspoon sugar

1½ tablespoons vegetable oil

2 garlic cloves, finely chopped

200 g (7 oz) oyster mushrooms, hard stalks removed, cut in half if large

200 g (7 oz) shiitake mushrooms, hard stalks removed

2 spring onions (scallions), sliced diagonally, for garnish

1 long red chilli, seeded and finely sliced, for garnish

1 Drain each block of tofu and cut into 2.5 cm (1 inch) pieces. Put them in a shallow dish and sprinkle with the sesame oil, light soy sauce, ground pepper and ginger. Leave to marinate for 30 minutes.

2 Mix the stock with the light soy sauce, cornflour and sugar in a small bowl until smooth.

3 Heat the oil in a wok or frying pan and stir-fry the garlic over a medium heat until light brown. Add all the mushrooms and stir-fry for 4 minutes or until the mushrooms are cooked.

4 Add the cornflour liquid, then carefully add the pieces of tofu and gently mix for 1 to 2 minutes. Taste, then adjust the seasoning if necessary.

5 Spoon onto a serving plate and sprinkle with spring onions, chilli slices and ground pepper.

CHICKPEA BURGERS

MAKES 6

CHICKPEA PATTIES

2 teaspoons olive oil

1 small onion, finely chopped

2 garlic cloves, crushed

2 x 400 g (14 oz) tins chickpeas, rinsed and drained

95 g (3½ oz/½ cup) cooked brown rice (see Note)

50 g (1¾ oz/⅓ cup) sun-dried tomatoes, chopped

SPICY YOGHURT DRESSING

200 g (7 oz) thick plain yoghurt

1 garlic clove, crushed

¼ teaspoon ground cumin

¼ teaspoon ground coriander

1 eggplant (aubergine), cut into 1 cm (½ inch) slices

olive oil, for brushing

1 large red onion, sliced into rings

2 large handfuls rocket (arugula) leaves

6 pieces Turkish bread

1 **To make the chickpea patties,** heat the oil in a frying pan and cook the onion over medium heat for 2 minutes, or until lightly golden. Add the garlic and cook for 1 more minute, then remove from the heat and allow to cool slightly. Put the onion mixture in a food processor with the chickpeas, rice and sun-dried tomato. Using a pulse action, process in short bursts until the mixture is combined and the chickpeas are broken up, but not completely mushy, scraping the bowl down with a spatula during processing. Season to taste, then shape the mixture into six patties about 8 cm (3¼ inches) in diameter. Place on a tray lined with plastic wrap, cover and refrigerate for 1 hour.

2 **Put all the spicy yoghurt dressing** ingredients in a small bowl and mix together well. Refrigerate until needed.

3 **Preheat a barbecue flat plate** to moderately hot. Brush the eggplant slices lightly on each side with oil, and toss a little oil through the onion rings. Cook the eggplant and onion on the hotplate until tender and lightly golden — the eggplant will need about 3–4 minutes each side, the onion about 5 minutes. Transfer the vegetables to a plate and set aside.

4 **Brush the top of the chickpea patties** lightly with oil, then put them face-down on the hotplate and cook for 3 minutes. Brush the top of the patties with a little oil, then turn and cook for a further 3 minutes, or until golden. They may stick, so ensure your spatula is well underneath before turning.

5 **While the chickpea patties are cooking,** arrange the rocket, barbecued eggplant and onion on the Turkish bread slices. Add the hot chickpea patties, dollop with some of the spicy yoghurt dressing and serve at once.

Note: You will need to cook about 55 g (1¾ oz/¼ cup) of brown rice for this recipe. If you like your Turkish bread toasted, lightly grill the slices on both sides on the edge of the flat plate while the patties are cooking.

CHANNA MASALA

SERVES 6

1 cup (220 g/7 oz) dried chickpeas

2 tablespoons oil

2 onions, finely chopped

2 large ripe tomatoes, chopped

½ teaspoon ground coriander (cilantro)

1 teaspoon ground cumin

1 teaspoon chilli powder

¼ teaspoon ground turmeric

1 tablespoon channa (chole) masala (see Note)

20 g (¾ oz) ghee or butter

1 small white onion, sliced

fresh mint and coriander (cilantro) leaves, to garnish

1 Place the chickpeas in a bowl, cover with water and leave to soak overnight.

2 Drain, rinse and place in a large saucepan. Cover with plenty of water and bring to the boil, then reduce the heat and simmer for 40 minutes, or until soft. Drain.

3 Heat the oil in a large saucepan, add the onion and cook over medium heat for 15 minutes, or until golden brown.

4 Add the chopped tomato, ground coriander and cumin, chilli powder, turmeric, channa (chole) masala and 500 ml (16 fl oz/2 cups) cold water, and cook for 10 minutes, or until the tomato is soft.

5 Add the chickpeas, season well with salt and cook for 7–10 minutes, or until the sauce thickens.

6 Transfer to a serving dish. Place the ghee or butter on top and allow to melt before serving. Garnish with sliced onion and fresh mint and coriander leaves.

Note: Channa (chole) masala is a spice blend specifically used in this dish. It is available at Indian grocery stores. Garam masala can be used as a substitute, but this will alter the final flavour.

MUSHROOM MOUSSAKA

SERVES 4–6

1 eggplant (about 250 g/8 oz), cut into 1 cm (½ inch) slices

1 large potato, cut into 1 cm (½ inch) slices

30 g (1 oz) butter

1 onion, finely chopped

2 cloves garlic, finely chopped

500 g (1 lb) flat mushrooms, sliced

400 g (13 oz) can chopped tomatoes

½ teaspoon sugar

40 g (1¼ oz) butter, extra

40 g (1¼ oz/⅓ cup) plain (all-purpose) flour

500 ml (16 fl oz/2 cups) milk

1 egg, lightly beaten

40 g (1¼ oz) grated parmesan cheese

1   **Preheat the oven to hot** 220°C (425°F/Gas 7). Line a large baking tray with foil and brush with oil. Put the eggplant and potato in a single layer on the tray and sprinkle with salt and freshly ground black pepper. Bake for 20 minutes.

2   **Melt the butter** in a large frying pan over medium heat. Add the onion and cook, stirring, for 3–4 minutes, or until soft. Add the garlic and cook for 1 minute, or until fragrant. Increase heat to high, add the mushrooms and stir continuously for 2–3 minutes, or until they are soft. Add the tomato, reduce the heat and simmer rapidly for 8 minutes, or until mixture is reduced. Stir in the sugar.

3   **Melt the extra butter** in a large saucepan over low heat. Add the flour and cook for 1 minute, or until pale and foaming. Remove from the heat and gradually stir in the milk. Return to the heat and stir constantly until it boils and thickens. Reduce the heat and simmer for 2 minutes. Remove from the heat and, when the bubbles subside, stir in the egg and parmesan.

4   **Reduce the oven** to moderate 180°C (350°F/Gas 4). Grease a shallow 1.5 litre (48 fl oz) ovenproof dish. Spoon one third of the mushroom mixture into the dish. Cover with potato and top with half the remaining mushrooms, then the eggplant. Finish with the remaining mushrooms, pour on the sauce and smooth the top. Bake for 30–35 minutes, or until the edges bubble. Leave for 10 minutes before serving.

ALOO GOBI

SERVES 4

GARAM MASALA
MAKES 3 TABLESPOONS

8 cardamom pods

2 Indian bay leaves (cassia leaves)

1 teaspoon black peppercorns

2 teaspoons cumin seeds

2 teaspoons coriander seeds

5 cm (2 inch) cinnamon stick

1 teaspoon cloves

3 tablespoons oil

½ teaspoon black mustard seeds

½ onion, finely chopped

200 g (7 oz) potatoes, cut into cubes

¼ teaspoon ground turmeric

1 teaspoon ground cumin

1 teaspoon ground coriander

1½ teaspoons garam masala (see Note)

4 ripe tomatoes, chopped

1 large cauliflower (about 1.25 kg/

2 lb 12 oz), cut into florets

2 cm (¾ inch) piece of ginger

1 teaspoon sugar

1 **To make the garam masala,** remove the seeds from the cardamom pods. Break the bay leaves into small pieces. Put them in a spice grinder or pestle and mortar with the remaining spices and grind to a fine powder.

2 **Heat the oil** in a karhai or deep, heavy-based frying pan over low heat. Add the mustard seeds, cover the pan and wait for the seeds to pop.

3 **Add the onion** and potato and fry until lightly browned. Add the turmeric, cumin, coriander and garam masala to the pan and fry for a couple of seconds.

4 **Add the tomato** and stir until the spices are well mixed. Add the cauliflower florets and stir until well mixed.

5 **Stir in the ginger,** sugar and 125 ml (½ cup) water, increase the heat to medium and bring to the boil. Reduce the heat, cover and simmer for 15 minutes, or until the vegetables are tender. Season with salt, to taste.

6 **Uncover the pan** and if the sauce is too runny, simmer it for another 1–2 minutes before serving. Serve hot with rice.

Note: Garam masala is best made fresh just before you begin cooking, but if you haven't got the patience, make a batch ahead and store for several months in an airtight container in a cool, dark place.

AROMATIC VEGETABLE AND CHICKPEA CURRY

SERVES 4

1 tablespoon peanut oil

1 onion, chopped

2 garlic cloves, crushed

1½ teaspoons ground cumin

1 teaspoon ground turmeric

1½ teaspoons ground coriander

1 green chilli, deseeded and chopped

2 all-purpose potatoes, chopped into
    4 cm (1½ inch) pieces

2 carrots, cut into 4 cm (1½ inch) pieces

400 g (14 oz) tinned chopped tomatoes

80 g (2¾ oz/½ cup) frozen peas

420 g (15 oz) tinned chickpeas,
    drained, rinsed

500 ml (17 fl oz/2 cups) vegetable stock

90 g (3¼ oz) baby English spinach
    leaves

SAFFRON AND CARDAMOM RICE

500 ml (17 fl oz/2 cups) vegetable stock

6–8 saffron threads

6 cardamom pods

400 g (14 oz/2 cups) basmati rice

1 Heat the oil in a saucepan over medium heat. Cook the onion and garlic, stirring, for 3 minutes, or until the onion is transparent.

2 Add the cumin, turmeric, coriander and chilli, and stir until the spices are fragrant.

3 Add the potatoes and carrots to the pan. Cook for about 1 minute, stirring to coat in the spice mix.

4 Stir in the tomatoes, peas, chickpeas and vegetable stock. Cover the saucepan with a lid. Cook for 20 minutes, stirring occasionally.

5 Stir in the spinach leaves and cook until the spinach is wilted. Season the curry with salt and freshly ground black pepper to taste.

6 To make the rice, bring the stock to the boil in a saucepan. Add the saffron, cardamom and rice. Bring the water back to the boil, reduce the heat to low, cover with a lid and steam the rice for 20 minutes. Remove from the heat. Fluff with a fork. Serve the curry with the rice.

BROWN RICE TART WITH TOMATO AND FETA

SERVES 6

200 g (7 oz/1 cup) brown rice

60 g (2 oz/½ cup) grated cheddar cheese

1 egg, lightly beaten

FILLING

6 roma (plum) tomatoes, halved

6 garlic cloves, unpeeled

1 tablespoon olive oil

8 lemon thyme sprigs

45 g (1½ oz/⅓ cup) crumbled feta or goat's cheese

3 eggs

60 ml (2 fl oz/¼ cup) milk

1 Boil the rice for 35–40 minutes, or until tender; drain and leave to cool. Meanwhile, preheat the oven to 200°C (400°F/Gas 6).

2 Put the rice, cheese and egg in a bowl and mix together well. Spread the mixture over the base and sides of a lightly greased 25 cm (10 inch) flan (tart) tin or quiche dish and bake for 15 minutes. Remove from the oven and set aside.

3 To make the filling, place the tomatoes on a non-stick baking tray, cut side up, along with the garlic. Brush with the olive oil and grind some black pepper over the top. Bake for 30 minutes, then remove from the oven and leave to cool slightly. Squeeze the garlic cloves out of their skins.

4 Reduce the oven temperature to 180°C (350°F/Gas 4). Arrange the tomato halves, garlic, lemon thyme sprigs and feta over the rice crust.

5 In a bowl, whisk together the eggs and milk, then pour over the tomatoes. Bake for 1 hour, or until the filling has set. Serve hot or cold.

PEA AND ASPARAGUS SAFFRON RISOTTO

SERVES 4

450 g (1 lb) fresh peas (in the pod), or 235 g (8½ oz/1½ cups) frozen peas

175 g (6 oz/1 bunch) asparagus

pinch saffron threads

2 tablespoons olive oil

1 onion, finely chopped

440 g (15½ oz/2 cups) risotto rice

1.5 litres (52 fl oz/6 cups) vegetable stock

30 g (1 oz) parmesan cheese, finely grated

1 **Shell the peas** into a heatproof bowl. Trim the woody ends from the asparagus, and cut the stalks into 3 cm (1¼ inch) lengths. Add to the bowl, and cover with boiling water. Stand for 3 minutes, then drain and set aside until needed. Put 3 tablespoons of boiling water into a small bowl, and add the saffron threads. Set aside until required.

2 **Heat the oil** in a large, heavy-based saucepan. Add the onion and cook over medium heat for 5 minutes, until soft and transparent. Add the rice and cook, stirring, for 1 minute, until glassy.

3 **Meanwhile,** put the stock into a smaller saucepan. Cover and bring to the boil, then reduce the heat to low and keep at a gentle simmer.

4 **Add about 4 tablespoons** of the hot stock to the rice, stirring constantly. When it has absorbed into the rice, add another 4 tablespoons of the hot stock. Keep adding stock, stirring between each addition, until the rice is tender and creamy. This will take about 25 minutes. Add the saffron and the liquid about halfway through adding the stock.

5 **About 5 minutes** before the rice is ready, add the peas and asparagus to the rice so that they will cook with the last addition of stock. Remove from the heat, and stir in the parmesan. Serve immediately, and top with freshly ground black pepper.

TAGLIATELLE WITH MUSHROOMS AND SAFFRON CREAM

SERVES 4

15 g (½ oz) dried porcini mushrooms

30 g (1 oz) butter

250 g (9 oz) swiss brown mushrooms, sliced

150 g (5½ oz) shiitake mushrooms, sliced

3 bulb spring onions (scallions), sliced

2 garlic cloves, crushed

125 ml (4 fl oz/½ cup) dry white wine

½ teaspoon saffron threads

¼ teaspoon cayenne pepper

300 ml (10½ fl oz) thick (double/heavy) cream

400 g (14 oz) fresh tagliatelle

2 tablespoons roughly snipped chives

grated parmesan cheese, to serve

1 Soak the porcini mushrooms in 3 tablespoons of water for 30 minutes. Remove from the liquid and slice, reserving the liquid.

2 In a large heavy-based frying pan, melt the butter over medium heat until foaming, then add all the mushrooms, spring onions and garlic, stirring, for 5 minutes. Add the white wine, reserved mushroom liquid, saffron threads, cayenne pepper and cream. Reduce the heat to low and simmer for 7 minutes, or until the sauce thickens slightly, stirring occasionally. Season to taste.

3 In a large saucepan, bring salted water to the boil and cook the pasta for 5–6 minutes, or until *al dente*. Strain the pasta in a colander.

4 Toss the pasta through the sauce and serve in bowls. Sprinkle each bowl with chopped chives and freshly ground black pepper. Serve with parmesan cheese.

ITALIAN ZUCCHINI PIE

SERVES 4–6

600 g (1 lb 5 oz) zucchini (courgettes), grated and mixed with ¼ teaspoon salt

150 g (5½ oz) provolone cheese, grated

120 g (4½ oz) ricotta cheese

3 eggs

2 garlic cloves, crushed

2 teaspoons finely chopped basil

pinch ground nutmeg

2 sheets ready-rolled shortcrust pastry

1 egg (extra), lightly beaten

1 Preheat the oven to 200°C (400°F/ Gas 6) and heat a baking tray. Grease a 23 cm (9 inch) (top) pie dish.

2 Drain the zucchini in a colander for 30 minutes, then squeeze out any excess liquid.

3 Place in a bowl with the cheeses, eggs, garlic, basil and nutmeg. Season and mix well.

4 Using two-thirds of the pastry, line the base and sides of the dish. Spoon the filling into the pastry shell and level the surface. Brush the exposed rim of the pastry with egg. Use two-thirds of the remaining pastry to make a lid and cover the filling with it, pressing the edges together firmly. Trim the edges and reserve the scraps. Crimp the rim. Prick the top all over with a skewer and brush with egg.

5 From the remaining pastry, cut a strip about 30 cm x 10 cm (12 inches x 4 inches). Cut this into nine lengths 1 cm (1/2 inch) wide. Press three ropes together at one end and press onto the workbench. Plait the ropes. Make two more plaits, trim the ends and space the plaits parallel across the centre of the pie.

6 Brush the top of the pie with the beaten egg to glaze. Bake on the hot tray for 50 minutes, or until golden. Serve hot or cold.

GNOCCHI WITH GORGONZOLA AND GOAT'S CHEESE SAUCE

SERVES 4

30 g (1 oz/¼ cup) roasted skinned
  hazelnuts

150 g (5½ oz) gorgonzola cheese or
  other strong dry blue cheese

100 g (3½ oz/¾ cup, heaped)
  goat's cheese

4 tablespoons thyme

grated zest of 1 lemon

750 g (1 lb 10 oz) potato gnocchi

80 ml (2½ fl oz/⅓ cup) extra virgin
  olive oil

2 leeks, white part only, thinly sliced

60 ml (2 fl oz/¼ cup) pouring cream

1 Put the hazelnuts in a mini processor and whizz in 2-second bursts for 20 seconds, or until roughly chopped. Transfer to a small bowl.

2 Put the gorgonzola or blue cheese, goat's cheese, thyme and lemon zest in the mini processor and whizz in short bursts for 15 seconds, or until crumbled.

3 Cook the potato gnocchi in a large saucepan of boiling salted water according to the manufacturer's instructions. Drain the gnocchi, return to the pan and toss with a little of the oil.

4 Meanwhile, heat 2 tablespoons of the oil in a large frying pan over medium–high heat, add the leek and sauté for 5–6 minutes, or until softened. Add the cream and the cheese mixture and cook, stirring, over low heat for 3–5 minutes, or until the cheese has melted.

5 Add the cheese sauce and remaining oil to the gnocchi and gently toss through. Season with salt and freshly ground black pepper, to taste.

6 Spoon into four bowls, sprinkle with the chopped hazelnuts and serve immediately.

LENTIL BHUJA CASSEROLE

SERVES 4–6

375 g (13 oz/2 cups) green lentils

1 large onion

1 large all-purpose potato

1 teaspoon ground cumin

1 teaspoon ground coriander

1 teaspoon ground turmeric

90 g (3¼ oz/¾ cup) plain (all-purpose) flour

vegetable oil, for pan-frying

2 garlic cloves, crushed

1 tablespoon grated fresh ginger

250 ml (9 fl oz/1 cup) tomato passata (puréed tomatoes)

500 ml (17 fl oz/2 cups) vegetable stock

250 ml (9 fl oz/1 cup) pouring cream

200 g (7 oz) green beans, trimmed

2 carrots, sliced

pitta bread, to serve

1 **Put the lentils** in a bowl, cover with cold water and leave to soak overnight. Drain well and place in a bowl.

2 **Grate the onion** and potato, place in a clean tea towel (dish towel) and squeeze out the excess moisture. Add to the lentils with the spices and flour and mix well. Using dry hands, roll the mixture into walnut-sized balls and place on a foil-lined tray. Cover and refrigerate for 30 minutes.

3 **Heat about 2 cm** (¾ inch) of oil in a heavy-based frying pan. Add the lentil balls in small batches and fry over high heat for 5 minutes, or until golden brown. Drain on paper towels.

4 **Heat another 2 tablespoons** oil in a large saucepan. Add the garlic and ginger and sauté over medium heat for 1 minute, then stir in the tomato passata, stock and cream. Bring to the boil, then reduce the heat and simmer for 10 minutes.

5 **Add the lentil balls,** beans and carrot. Cover and simmer for 35 minutes, stirring occasionally.

6 **Serve** hot, with pitta bread.

Note: The lentil balls can be made a day ahead and stored in an airtight container in the refrigerator.

IDIYAPPAM

SERVES 4

225 g (8 oz) rice stick noodles

80 ml (2½ fl oz/⅓ cup) vegetable oil

50 g (1¾ oz/⅓ cup) cashew nuts

1/2 onion, chopped

150 g (5½ oz/1 cup) fresh or frozen peas

10 curry leaves

2 carrots, grated

2 leeks, white part only, finely shredded

1 red capsicum (pepper), diced

2 tablespoons tomato sauce (ketchup)

1 tablespoon soy sauce

1 teaspoon sea salt

3 hard-boiled eggs, peeled and cut into
    wedges

1 Soak the noodles in cold water for 30 minutes, then drain and place in a saucepan of boiling water. Remove from the heat and stand for 3 minutes, then drain and refresh in cold water.

2 Heat 1 tablespoon of the oil in a wok. Add the cashews and fry over medium heat until golden. Remove and set aside.

3 Add the onion to the wok and stir-fry for 7 minutes, or until dark golden. Remove and drain on paper towels.

4 Meanwhile, cook the peas in boiling water until tender. Drain and keep warm.

5 Heat the remaining oil in the wok over medium heat. Briefly fry the curry leaves, then add the carrot, leek and capsicum and stir for 1 minute.

6 Add the tomato sauce, soy sauce, salt and noodles and cook until heated through, stirring constantly so the noodles don't stick.

7 Pile the noodles onto a platter and serve garnished with the peas, cashews, fried onion and egg.

FRAGRANT VEGETABLES WITH COUSCOUS

SERVES 4

2 tablespoons olive oil

1 large onion, chopped

2 garlic cloves, crushed

1 tablespoon finely grated fresh ginger

2 teaspoons ground cumin

2 teaspoons ground coriander

½ teaspoon cayenne pepper

½ teaspoon Hungarian sweet paprika

400 g (14 oz) tinned chopped tomatoes

250 ml (9 fl oz/1 cup) vegetable stock

1 swede, peeled and cut into
   3 cm (1¼ inch) chunks

2 carrots, peeled, quartered and cut into
   3 cm (1¼ inch) lengths

400 g (14 oz) orange sweet potato,
   peeled and cut into 3 cm (1¼ inch)
   chunks

2 zucchini (courgettes), cut into 2 cm
   (¾ inch) slices

270 g (9½ oz/1½ cups) couscous

1 Heat 1 **tablespoon** of the olive oil in a large heavy-based saucepan. Add the onion and cook over medium heat for 10 minutes, stirring occasionally, or until very soft and golden.

2 Add the **garlic,** ginger, cumin, coriander, cayenne and paprika and cook, stirring, for 1 minute.

3 Add the **tomatoes** and stock, and stir, scraping the bottom of the pan. Add the swede and carrot, cover and bring to the boil. Reduce the heat to low and simmer, covered, for 15 minutes.

4 Add the **sweet potato** and cook for a further 30 minutes, then add the zucchini. Cook for 15–20 minutes, or until the vegetables are tender. Season to taste.

5 Put 500 ml (17 fl oz/2 cups) of water and the remaining olive oil into a saucepan, cover and bring to the boil. Add the couscous, turn off the heat and stand for 5 minutes. Uncover and fluff up the grains with a fork.

6 **To serve,** divide the couscous between warmed serving bowls, and top with the vegetables and their liquid.

VEGETABLE CASSEROLE WITH HERB DUMPLINGS

SERVES 4

1 tablespoon olive oil

1 large onion, chopped

2 garlic cloves, crushed

2 teaspoons sweet paprika

1 large all-purpose potato, chopped

1 large carrot, sliced

400 g (14 oz) tin chopped tomatoes

375 ml (13 fl oz/1½ cups) vegetable stock

400 g (14 oz) orange sweet potato, peeled and diced

150 g (5½ oz/2½ cups) broccoli florets

2 zucchini (courgettes), thickly sliced

2 tablespoons sour cream

HERB DUMPLINGS

125 g (4½ oz/1 cup) self-raising flour

20 g (¾ oz) cold butter, chopped

2 teaspoons chopped flat-leaf (Italian) parsley

1 teaspoon thyme

1 teaspoon chopped rosemary

80 ml (2½ fl oz/⅓ cup) milk

1 Preheat the oven to 200°C (400°F/Gas 6).

2 Heat the olive oil in a large saucepan. Sauté the onion over medium heat for 5 minutes, or until soft.

3 Add the garlic and paprika and cook, stirring, for 1 minute.

4 Add the potato, carrot, tomato and stock. Bring to the boil, then reduce the heat, cover and simmer for 10 minutes.

5 Add the sweet potato, broccoli and zucchini and simmer for a further 10 minutes, or until all the vegetables are tender.

6 Meanwhile, make the dumplings. Sift the flour and a pinch of salt into a bowl. Lightly rub in the butter with your fingertips until the mixture resembles fine breadcrumbs. Stir in the herbs and make a well in the centre. Add the milk and mix using a flat-bladed knife until the mixture comes together in beads. Gather up the dough and lift onto a lightly floured surface. Divide into eight portions, then shape each into a ball.

7 Stir the sour cream into the casserole. Transfer to a 2 litre (70 fl oz/8 cup) baking dish and top with the dumplings.

8 Bake for 20 minutes, or until the dumplings are golden and cooked. Serve hot.

ORECCHIETTE WITH SPICED PUMPKIN AND YOGHURT

SERVES 6

21 kg (2 lb 4 oz) pumpkin or butternut
   pumpkin (squash), cut into 2 cm
   (¾ inch) cubes

80 ml (⅓ cup) olive oil

500 g (1 lb 2 oz) orecchiette (see Note)

2 garlic cloves, crushed

1 teaspoon dried chilli flakes

1 teaspoon coriander seeds, crushed

1 tablespoon cumin seeds, crushed

185 g (¾ cup) thick natural yoghurt

3 tablespoons chopped coriander
   (cilantro) leaves

1   Preheat the oven to 200°C (400°F/Gas 6). Toss the pumpkin cubes in 2 tablespoons of the oil, place in a roasting tin and cook for 30 minutes, or until golden and crisp, tossing halfway through.

2   Meanwhile, cook the pasta in a large saucepan of boiling salted water until *al dente*. Drain and return to the pan.

3   Heat the remaining oil in a saucepan. Add the garlic, chilli, coriander and cumin and cook for 30 seconds, or until fragrant. Toss the spice mix and pumpkin through the pasta, then stir in the yoghurt and coriander and season to taste with salt and freshly ground black pepper. Divide among serving bowls.

Note: Orecchiette means 'little ears' in Italian, and the name of the pasta is a literal description of the shape — although some brands look more like curls than ears. If unavailable, you can use conchiglie or cavatelli.

EGGPLANT AND COCONUT CURRY

SERVES 6

500 g (1 lb 2 oz) slim eggplants (aubergines), trimmed and cut into 3 cm (1¼ inch) chunks
4 tablespoons vegetable oil
1 tablespoon panch phora (see Note)
2 teaspoons ground cumin
1 teaspoon ground turmeric
1 red onion, finely sliced
3 garlic cloves, chopped
1 long green chilli, deseeded and finely chopped
8 dried curry leaves (see Note)
400 ml (14 fl oz) coconut milk

1 Put the eggplant in a colander and sprinkle with salt. Set aside for 15 minutes to sweat. Rinse, drain and pat dry with paper towel.

2 Heat 2 tablespoons of the oil in a large heavy-based non-stick frying pan. Fry the eggplant for 5 minutes, stirring frequently, or until lightly browned. Remove to a side plate.

3 Heat the remaining oil in the frying pan. Add the panch phora, cumin and turmeric and cook for 1 minute, or until the mixture is aromatic.

4 Add the onion and cook for 3 minutes, or until the onion is cooked.

5 Stir in the garlic, chilli and curry leaves and add the eggplant. Stir to coat in the spices.

6 Stir in the coconut milk and 250 ml (9 fl oz/1 cup) of water. Season with salt.

7 Cook, stirring frequently, for 20 minutes, or until the eggplant is cooked and the sauce is thick. Serve hot or at room temperature.

Note: Panch phora is an Indian spice that incorporates the flavours of fenugreek, cumin, fennel, mustard and nigella seeds. Dried curry leaves are available from Asian food stores and some large supermarkets.

CORN SPOONBREAD

3 cobs of sweet corn

250 g (9 oz/1 cup) crème fraîche

1 egg

30 g (1 oz/¼ cup) self-raising flour

a pinch of cayenne pepper

50 g (1¾ oz/½ cup) grated parmesan
   cheese

40 g (1½ oz) butter

1 **Preheat the oven** to 190°C (375°F/Gas 5).

2 **Slice the kernels** off the corn cobs and place in a large bowl.

3 **Add the crème fraîche,** egg, flour, cayenne pepper and half the parmesan. Season with sea salt and freshly ground black pepper and mix together well.

4 **Spoon the mixture into a greased,** shallow 18 cm (7 inch) baking dish. Sprinkle the remaining parmesan over the top, dot with the butter and bake for 30–35 minutes, or until firm and golden brown. Serve hot, straight from the dish.

DHAL WITH VEGETABLES

SERVES 6

150 g (5½ oz/⅔ cup) yellow lentils

150 g (5½ oz/scant ⅔ cup) red lentils

1 tablespoon ghee

1 onion, chopped

2 garlic cloves, crushed

1 tablespoon fenugreek seeds

2 teaspoons ground cumin

2 teaspoons ground coriander

½ teaspoon ground turmeric

400 g (14 oz) tin chopped tomatoes

750 ml (26 fl oz/3 cups) vegetable stock

2 carrots, chopped

250 g (9 oz/2 cups) cauliflower florets

150 g (5½ oz/1¼ cups) green beans, trimmed and halved

3 tablespoons cream

2 tablespoons chopped coriander (cilantro) leaves

naan bread, to serve

1 **Rinse the lentils,** separately, under cold water until the water runs clear, then drain well. Put the yellow lentils in a small bowl, cover with water and stand for 30 minutes, then drain well.

2 **Heat the ghee** in a saucepan over medium heat.

3 **Add the onion** and garlic, stirring, for about 3 minutes, or until the onion is soft.

4 **Stir in the spices and cook,** stirring, for about 30 seconds, or until fragrant.

5 **Add the lentils,** tomatoes and stock. Bring to the boil over high heat, then reduce the heat to low and simmer, covered, for 20 minutes.

6 **Stir in the carrots and cauliflower.** Cover and cook for 10 minutes.

7 **Add the beans** and cook, covered, for a further 5 minutes, or until the lentils are tender and the vegetables are cooked. Season to taste. Stir in the cream.

8 **Serve** the dhal sprinkled with the coriander leaves and accompanied by naan bread.

DESSERTS

LEMON AND LIME CURDS

MAKES 6

4 eggs

2 egg yolks

175 g (6 oz/¾ cup) caster
   (superfine) sugar

100 ml (3½ fl oz) lemon juice

2½ tablespoons lime juice

finely grated zest of 2 limes

300 ml (10½ fl oz) thick (double/heavy)
   cream

boiling water, for steaming

baby meringues, to serve

thick (double/heavy) cream, to serve

candied lemons

115 g (4 oz/½ cup) caster (superfine)
   sugar

1 lemon, finely sliced

1   Preheat the oven to 160°C (315°F/Gas 2–3). Line a roasting tin with a tea towel (dish towel), then place six 185 ml (6 fl oz/¾ cup) ramekins in the tin.

2   Combine the eggs, egg yolks and sugar in a large bowl and whisk until the sugar has dissolved and the mixture is well combined. Stir in the lemon and lime juice and the lime zest. Add the cream and mix well to combine. Pour the mixture into the ramekins, then pour enough boiling water into the roasting tin to come halfway up the side of the ramekins.

3   Bake for 30 minutes, or until just set (the curds should be slightly wobbly when you shake them). Remove the ramekins from the roasting tin and allow to cool. Refrigerate until cold.

4   Meanwhile, to make the candied lemons, put the sugar and 125 ml (4 fl oz/½ cup) of water in a saucepan over medium–high heat and stir until the sugar has dissolved. Add the lemon slices and bring to the boil. Reduce the heat to medium and simmer without stirring for 5–10 minutes, or until the syrup has reduced a little. Remove from the heat and allow to cool. Chill in the refrigerator until ready to serve.

5   Place a candied lemon slice on top of each curd and drizzle with some of the syrup. Serve with baby meringues and thick cream.

CARROT AND GINGER SYRUP PUDDING

SERVES 6

60 g (2¼ oz) unsalted butter, softened

55 g (2 oz/¼ cup) soft brown sugar

55 g (2 oz/¼ cup) caster (superfine) sugar

2 eggs

4 tablespoons milk

80 g (2¾ oz/½ cup) grated carrot

2 tablespoons finely chopped glacé ginger

90 g (3¼ oz/¾ cup) self-raising flour

½ teaspoon bicarbonate of soda (baking soda)

½ teaspoon mixed spice

2 tablespoons golden syrup or maple syrup

cream, ice cream or custard, to serve

1 **Press a large piece** of baking paper over the base and into the corners of a 20 cm (8 inch) steamer. Pleat the paper up the sides and allow the paper to overlap the top edges. Spray or brush with olive oil.

2 **Using electric beaters,** beat the butter, brown sugar and caster sugar in a large bowl until thick and creamy, scraping down the sides of the bowl as you go. Beat in the eggs, one at a time.

3 **Stir in the milk,** carrot and ginger. Add the sifted flour, bicarbonate of soda and mixed spice and stir lightly until the mixture is combined.

4 **Pour the mixture** into the steamer and cover with a lid. Sit the steamer over a saucepan or wok of boiling water and steam for 30 minutes, or until the pudding is firm in the centre. Lift out and drizzle the golden syrup over the top.

5 **Cut into wedges** and serve hot or at room temperature with cream, ice cream or custard.

STICKY RICE WITH MANGO

SERVES 4

200 g (7 oz/1 cup) sticky rice

170 ml (6 fl oz/⅔ cup) coconut milk

1 tablespoon palm sugar (not too brown)

½ teaspoon salt

4 large ripe mangoes

170 ml (6 fl oz/⅔ cup) can coconut cream mixed with ¼ teaspoon salt, for garnish

1 **To make the sticky rice with coconut milk,** put the rice in a bowl and pour in cold water to come 5 cm (2 inches) above the rice. Soak for at least 3 hours, or overnight. Drain and transfer to a bamboo basket specially made for steaming sticky rice, or to a steamer lined with a double thickness of muslin. Spread the rice in the steamer. Bring the water in the bottom of the steamer to a rolling boil. Taking care, set the rice over the water. Lower the heat, cover and steam for 20 to 25 minutes or until the rice swells and is glistening and tender. The cooking time will vary depending on the soaking time. Check and replenish the water every 10 minutes or so.

2 **While the rice is cooking,** stir the coconut milk, sugar and salt in a seperate small saucepan over low heat until the sugar has dissolved.

3 **As soon as the rice is cooked,** use a wooden spoon to gently mix it with the coconut milk. Set aside for 15 minutes.

4 **Meanwhile,** peel the mangoes and slice off the two outside cheeks of each, removing as much flesh as you can in large pieces. Avoid cutting very close to the stone where the flesh is fibrous. Discard the stone. Slice each cheek lengthways into four or five pieces.

5 **To serve,** arrange the mango pieces on a serving plate. Spoon a portion of steamed sticky rice with coconut milk near the mango slices. Spoon the coconut cream garnish on top and serve at room temperature.

BAKED ALMOND AND MARZIPAN PEACHES

SERVES 6

3 large ripe, firm peaches

40 g (1½ oz/⅓ cup) roughly chopped dark chocolate

50 g (1¾ oz/⅓ cup) whole blanched almonds, toasted and chopped

2½ tablespoons marzipan, chopped

2 tablespoons caster (superfine) sugar

1½ tablespoons unsalted butter, softened

1 egg yolk, lightly beaten

crème anglaise or thick (double/heavy) cream, to serve

CRÈME ANGLAISE
MAKES ABOUT 500 ML (17 FL OZ/2 CUPS)

4 egg yolks

115 g (4 oz/½ cup) caster (superfine) sugar

200 ml (7 fl oz) milk

200 ml (7 fl oz) pouring cream

1 vanilla bean (alternatively, if you don't have a vanilla bean, substitute 1 teaspoon natural vanilla extract)

1 Preheat the oven to 170°C (325°F/Gas 3). Lightly grease a roasting tin or large ceramic ovenproof dish.

2 Cut the peaches in half on either side of the stone and set aside. Remove any remaining flesh from the stone and finely chop. Combine in a bowl with the remaining ingredients, stirring well.

3 Place the peaches, skin side down, in the tin. Divide the stuffing mixture among the peaches, pressing the mixture firmly onto the peach, heaping the mixture slightly if necessary.

4 Bake the peaches for 30 minutes, or until the peaches have softened and the filling is bubbling.

5 To make the crème anglaise, whisk the egg yolks and caster (superfine) sugar in a bowl until thick and pale. Combine the milk and pouring cream in a saucepan. Split 1 vanilla bean in half, scrape out the seeds and add the bean and seeds to the saucepan. Slowly bring almost to the boil. Strain the milk mixture onto the egg yolk mixture, stirring to combine. Discard the vanilla bean. Return mixture to a clean saucepan, then cook over medium–low heat, stirring constantly with a wooden spoon until mixture is thick enough to coat the back of the spoon. Do not allow custard to boil or it will curdle.

6 Cool slightly, then serve warm or at room temperature with thick cream or crème anglaise. To chill, lay plastic wrap directly on the surface of the custard to prevent a skin forming. Refrigerate for up to 2 days.

CARDAMOM, ORANGE AND PLUM DESSERT CAKES

MAKES 8

185 g (6½ oz) unsalted butter, chopped

95 g (3¼ oz/½ cup) soft brown sugar

115 g (4 oz/½ cup) caster (superfine) sugar

3 eggs

1 teaspoon finely grated orange zest

310 g (11 oz/2½ cups) self-raising flour, sifted

1 teaspoon ground cardamom

185 ml (6 fl oz/¾ cup) milk

4 tinned plums, drained and patted dry, cut in half

1 tablespoon raw (demerara) sugar

thick (double/heavy) cream or ice cream, to serve

1   **Preheat the oven** to 180°C (350°F/Gas 4). Lightly grease eight 250 ml (9 fl oz/1 cup) ceramic ramekins and dust with flour, shaking out any excess flour.

2   **Cream the butter** and sugars in a bowl using electric beaters until pale and fluffy. Add the eggs, one at a time and beating well after each addition, then stir in the orange zest.

3   **Fold the flour** and cardamom into the butter mixture alternately with the milk until combined and smooth.

4   **Divide the mixture** between the ramekins and place a plum half, cut side down, on top of the batter. Sprinkle with raw sugar, place the ramekins on a baking tray and bake for 30–35 minutes, or until golden and firm to the touch.

5   **Serve warm** or at room temperature with thick cream or ice cream.

BAKED PEARS IN SPICED SAUTERNES SYRUP

SERVES 6

250 ml (9 fl oz/1 cup) Sauternes or any dessert wine

345 g (12 oz/1½ cups) caster (superfine) sugar

2 cardamom pods, bruised

2 cloves

1 cinnamon stick

1 star anise

1 teaspoon rosewater

1 small piece of lemon rind, white pith removed

6 corella (or other small) pears, peeled

125 ml (4 fl oz/½ cup) Greek-style yoghurt, to serve

1 tablespoon honey, to serve

1 **Preheat the oven** to 180°C (350°F/Gas 4).

2 **Combine** 750 ml (26 fl oz/3 cups) water with the Sauternes, sugar, cardamom, cloves, cinnamon stick, star anise, rosewater and lemon rind in a saucepan. Stir over medium heat for 4–5 minutes, or until the sugar dissolves. Bring the mixture to the boil, then reduce the heat to low and cook for 8 minutes, or until the syrup has reduced by half.

3 **Halve the pears,** place them in a roasting tin and pour over the syrup. Cover with foil and bake for 20 minutes. Remove the foil, baste the pears with the syrup, then cook for a further 20 minutes, or until the pears are tender.

4 **Serve the pears** warm or at room temperature with the yoghurt and a little honey spooned over.

ROASTED SPICED PEARS AND STRAWBERRIES

SERVES 4

1 tablespoon melted unsalted butter

170 g (6 oz/¾ cup) caster (superfine) sugar

2 vanilla beans, split lengthways

2 star anise

1 cinnamon stick, broken in half

4 firm pears, peeled and cut into quarters

250 g (9 oz/1⅔ cups) strawberries, hulled, cut in half if large

Greek-style yoghurt, to serve

1 **Preheat the oven to 170°C** (325°F/Gas 3). Put 310 ml (10¾ fl oz/1¼ cups) of water, and the sugar, vanilla beans, star anise and cinnamon in an ovenproof dish. Place in the oven and cook for 10 minutes, stirring once, until the sugar dissolves.

2 **Add the pears** to the syrup. Cover with foil and cook for 35–45 minutes, or until almost tender, turning once in the syrup.

3 **Add the strawberries** and turn to coat in the syrup. Cover with foil and cook for a further 5 minutes, or until the strawberries soften.

4 **Set aside to cool.** Serve with yoghurt.

BANANA AND PLUM CRUMBLE

SERVES 4–6

30 g (1 oz/¼ cup) plain (all-purpose) flour

50 g (1¾ oz/½ cup) rolled oats

30 g (1 oz/½ cup) shredded coconut

45 g (1¾ oz/¼ cup) lightly packed soft brown sugar

finely grated zest from 1 lime

100 g (3½ oz) unsalted butter, cut into cubes

2 bananas, peeled and halved lengthways

4 plums, halved and stoned

60 ml (2 fl oz/¼ cup) lime juice

ice cream or whipped cream, to serve

1 Preheat the oven to 180°C (350°F/Gas 4).

2 Combine the flour, rolled oats, coconut, sugar and zest in a small bowl. Add the butter and, using your fingertips, rub the butter into the flour mixture until crumbly.

3 Put the bananas and plums in a 1.25 litre (44 fl oz/5 cup) capacity ovenproof dish and pour over the lime juice. Toss to coat in juice. Sprinkle crumble mixture evenly over the fruit.

4 Bake for 25–30 minutes, or until the crumble is golden. Serve hot with ice cream or whipped cream.

SPICED CARAMELIZED BANANAS

SERVES 4

50 g (1¾ oz) unsalted butter

2 tablespoons soft brown sugar

½ teaspoon ground nutmeg

¼ teaspoon ground allspice

4 bananas, peeled and sliced
    lengthways

grated zest and juice of 1 orange

1 tablespoon rum

2 tablespoons lightly roasted pecans or
    walnuts, chopped

freshly grated nutmeg, to sprinkle

ice cream, to serve

1 Put the butter, sugar, nutmeg and allspice in a frying pan over medium heat. Mix until combined and cook for 1 minute, or until the sugar has dissolved.

2 Add the bananas, cut side down, and cook for 2 minutes, or until a little softened. Remove to a serving plate.

3 Add orange zest and juice to the frying pan and stir for 2 minutes, or until mixture thickens and is syrupy. Add rum.

4 Spoon the sauce over the bananas. Sprinkle with the chopped nuts and sprinkle with some freshly grated nutmeg. Serve warm with ice cream..

NASHI AND GINGER STRUDEL

SERVES 6–8

4 small nashi pears, peeled, cored and sliced

1 tablespoon lemon juice

2 teaspoons fresh ginger, finely grated

30 g (1 oz/½ cup) panko (Japanese breadcrumbs)

230 g (8 oz/1 cup) caster (superfine) sugar

40 g (1½ oz/¼ cup) sesame seeds, lightly toasted, plus extra to garnish

50 g (1¾ oz/½ cup) walnuts, very finely chopped

1½ teaspoons ground cinnamon

1 teaspoon ground ginger

8 sheets filo pastry

150 g (5½ oz) unsalted butter, melted

2 tablespoons icing (confectioners') sugar

2 tablespoons kinako (roasted soya bean flour)

ice cream, to serve

---

1 Preheat the oven to 180°C (350°F/Gas 4). Lightly grease a baking tray.

2 Put the nashi slices in a bowl with the lemon juice, fresh ginger, panko and half the sugar and stir well.

3 Combine the sesame seeds, walnuts, cinnamon, ground ginger and remaining sugar in a separate bowl.

4 Lay one sheet of filo on a work surface with the long edge towards you, brush lightly with a little melted butter, then lay another sheet on top so it overlaps the edge furthest away from you by about 5 cm (2 in). Brush with a little more butter.

5 Sprinkle about one-quarter of the sesame mixture over the top of the two pastry sheets, then keep layering in the same position with the rest of the filo and sesame mix, brushing each sheet of pastry with melted butter. Leave a

4 cm (1½ in) border along the edge of the pastry closest to you and on both sides, and place the nashi mixture in a neat log along the edge closest to you. Carefully roll up, folding in the sides about halfway along, then continue rolling to the end.

6 Carefully transfer the strudel to the prepared tray, seam side down, and brush all over with melted butter. Bake for 50 minutes, or until golden.

7 Allow to cool slightly before sprinkling with sifted combined icing sugar and kinako.

8 Slice on the diagonal and serve with lightly whipped cream, if desired.

VEGETARIAN BASICS

CREAMY CHILLI DIPPING SAUCE

160 g (5¾ oz/⅔ cup) sour cream

3 tablespoons sweet chilli sauce

2 spring onions (scallions), finely chopped

2 tablespoons coriander (cilantro), chopped

1 tablespoon lime juice

1 To make the creamy chilli dipping sauce, put the sour cream in a bowl, add the sweet chilli sauce and stir to combine. Stir in the finely chopped spring onions (scallions), chopped coriander (cilantro) and lime juice. Mix well, then transfer to a serving dish.

2 **Chill** before serving.

HERB, GARLIC & YOGHURT DIPPING SAUCE

200 g (6½ oz) low-fat natural yoghurt

4 tablespoons skim milk

1 teaspoon Dijon mustard

1 tablespoon chives, finely chopped

2 teaspoons fresh parsley, finely chopped

2 teaspoons fresh oregano, chopped

1 clove garlic, crushed

1 To make the herb, garlic and yoghurt dipping sauce, put all the ingredients in a bowl and whisk together. Season with salt and freshly ground black pepper, to taste, then transfer to a serving dish.

2 **Chill** before serving.

HUMMUS DIPPING SAUCE

425 g (14 oz) can chickpeas

185 ml (6 fl oz/¾ cup) vegetable stock

1 tablespoon tahini paste

2 cloves garlic, chopped

1 teaspoon ground coriander

1 teaspoon ground cumin

2 tablespoons lemon juice

1 To make the hummus dipping sauce, drain the can of chickpeas and put in a food processor with the vegetable stock, tahini paste and chopped garlic.

2 **Stir the ground** coriander and cumin in a dry frying pan over medium heat for 3 minutes, or until aromatic. Cool slightly, add to the processor and mix until nearly smooth. Mix in the lemon juice.

3 **Season with** freshly ground black pepper and salt, to taste. If too thick, add a little water.

4 **Serve** at room temperature.

RICE VINEGAR & CHILLI DIPPING SAUCE

100 ml (3½ fl oz) rice vinegar

3 tablespoons sugar

pinch of salt

1 small red chilli, seeded and sliced

1 small green chilli, seeded and sliced

1 To make the rice vinegar and chilli dipping sauce, put the rice vinegar in a small saucepan. Add the sugar and a good pinch of salt. Bring slowly to the boil to dissolve the sugar.

2 **Leave to cool slightly,** then stir in the seeded and sliced small red chilli and the seeded and sliced small green chilli.

3 **Transfer** to a serving dish and leave to cool completely before serving.

1 **To make the peanut sauce,** take an unshaken 400 ml (14 fl oz) tin of coconut milk and scoop off the thick part that forms at the top (if there is none, just use about 3 tablespoons of coconut milk). Put it in a frying pan over medium heat.

2 **Add the red curry paste** and tomato paste (purée) and stir-fry for 2 minutes, or until aromatic. Add the remaining coconut milk, 2 tablespoons of peanut butter and 70 g (2½ oz/½ cup) of ground peanuts. Simmer gently over low heat, stirring, for 3 minutes.

3 **Leave to cool** before serving as a dipping sauce or use as a marinade on barbecued vegetable skewers.

PEANUT SAUCE

400 ml (14 fl oz) tin coconut milk

2½ tablespoons red curry paste

1 tablespoon tomato paste (purée)

2 tablespoons peanut butter

70 g (2½ oz/½ cup) ground peanuts

1 **To make the roasted capsicum dipping sauce,** quarter the capsicums, remove the seeds and membrane and grill (broil) until the skins blister and blacken. Cool under a damp tea towel (dish towel) before peeling. Cut one quarter into thin strips then set aside.

2 **Heat the oil** in a small pan, add the finely chopped spring onions and water, then stir over heat until the spring onion is soft. Add the remaining capsicum, stock, white wine, tomato paste and sugar. Simmer for 2 minutes, then blend until smooth.

3 **Season with** freshly ground black pepper and salt, to taste, stir in the chopped chives and garnish with red capsicum strips.

ROASTED CAPSICUM DIPPING SAUCE

2 red capsicums (peppers)

1 teaspoon oil, for frying

2 spring onions, finely chopped

1 tablespoon water

3 tablespoons vegetable stock

2 tablespoons white wine

2 tablespoons tomato paste

¼ teaspoon sugar

1 tablesppon chives, chopped

1 **To make the sweet cucumber dipping sauce,** put rice vinegar in a small saucepan with sugar and a pinch of salt. Bring slowly to the boil to dissolve the sugar.

2 **Leave to cool,** then stir in a diced cucumber, diced carrot and finely chopped coriander (cilantro) leaves.

3 **Transfer** to a serving dish.

SWEET CUCUMBER DIPPING SAUCE

3 tablespoons rice vinegar

2 tablespoons sugar

pinch of salt

5 cm (2 inch) piece of cucumber, diced

5 cm (2 inch) piece of carrot, diced

1 tablespoon coriander (cilantro) leaves, finely chopped

1 **To make the yoghurt dipping sauce,** beat all the ingredients in a small bowl until well combined.

2 **Cover bowl** with plastic wrap and refrigerate until needed.

YOGHURT DIPPING SAUCE

200 g (6½ oz) natural yoghurt

2 tablespoons onion, finely grated

½ teaspoon dried mint leaves

½ teaspoon salt

¼ teaspoon ground coriander

pinch ground cumin

INDEX